Daily Devotional

Steven M. Hitchcock

Columbus, Ohio

ACKNOWLEDGEMENTS

Special thanks to God for the inspiration, my wife Fawn, mother-in-law Julie and son Trey for everything they do, Beth B. for blessing me with her wonderful editing, and Bill and Linda F. for their continued encouragement and support.

Thanks to my mentors Greg L., and John P. for their guidance and leadership in my daily walk with God.

Thanks to all my family, friends, church family, and small group supporters who have been an ongoing encouragement in the faith.

Trish,

My hope is you will find deep meaning in the devotions as you read. May 2022 and beyond be filled with closeness to God. See God working in and around you and remember Ephesians 6:10 NIV " Be strong in the LORD and in HIS mighty power."

God Bless,

CONTENTS

January

January 1st

Prayer of the Week

Ephesians 1:18 (NIV)

"I pray that the eyes of your heart may be enlightened in order that you may know the hope to which He has called you, the riches of His glorious inheritance in His holy people."

As a new year begins, let's all pray for one another the prayer that Paul prayed to the people of Ephesus. May each person throughout the entire world know in their hearts the wonders and glory of God.

January 2nd

New Beginnings

The new year is here. Looking back at your year in review, think of the times that God helped you overcome obstacles and fears.

This new year will undoubtedly bring new challenges and great rewards. Making resolutions and goals can help you face the new chapter of your life.

The Bible tells us in Psalm 118:14 (NASB): *"The Lord is my strength and song, and He has become my salvation."*

In this new year, be grateful that God has given you victory over many things over the past year.

January 3rd

GPS

Many of you have heard of GPS or global positioning system which uses satellites to let you know where you are located throughout the world. Some vehicles come with them preinstalled and watercraft use them to navigate in open waters too.

Perhaps you've heard of the other more, powerful GPS - God's Positioning System? My will for my life has gotten me way off God's course for my life. When I trust myself and deviate from God's plan, I get lost often. Much like a Global Positioning System, it knows the best path and you end up lost when you trust yourself. You can get back on track by trusting and following God.

The Bible says in Psalms 143:10 (NASB): *"Teach me to do Your will, for You are my God; lead me on level ground."*

Following God's will for your life will prevent you from being lost.

January 4th

God's Will, Not Mine

Whose will do you serve in your life? Whose will be best for your life? Most likely you think that you know what's best for you. I used to think that way. Once I started to understand that God knows what's best for me, I started to stop seeking my own interests.

Jesus tells us in Matthew 7:7 (NASB): *"Ask, and it will be given to you; seek and you will find; knock and it will be opened to you."*

God has much greater plans for you, if you follow His will for your life.

January 5th

Chasing Peace

Like me, many people find themselves chasing after peace. There are plenty of podcasts and programs that promise an outline to finding peace in your life.

I have tried various methods of finding peace and the best one is starting my day with a "God Cast" to prepare me for what today might bring. God Cast is simply getting into the word of God through reading the Bible – or devotionals like this one.

Jesus says in John 14:27 (NASB): *"Peace I leave with you; My peace I give to you; not as the world gives do, I give to you. Do not let your heart be troubled nor let it be fearful."*

Find a way to tune into God and He will help you find true Peace.

January 6th

Don't Laugh

Has God told you something and you laughed it off as if that would never happen? You wouldn't be the first and won't be the last to do so.

Sarah laughed at the thought of having a child due to her old age. God chose to bless Sarah with a child (Gn 18:12 New American Standard Bible).

Jesus says Luke 18:27(NASB): *"But He said, 'The things that are impossible with people are possible with God."*

Listen to what God is telling you and take it to heart because what He says is no laughing matter.

January 7th

The Light that Shines Bright

Have you ever been walking a path at night when it's tough to see the step in front of you? It's like maneuvering through life with no clear direction.

Maybe you are not on the path God has planned for you. I have been in this situation more times than I would like to count. The more I allow God to steer my direction, the path is well lit.

The Bible says in Psalms 119:105 (NASB): *"Your word is a lamp to my feet and a light to my path."*

Be encouraged to allow God to light your path. It is easier to navigate when the path is visible.

January 8th

Prayer of the Week

1 John 5:14 (NLT)

"And we are confident that He hears us whenever we ask for anything that pleases Him."

Practice praying for God's will instead of your own will for by praying in this manner you can rest assured that God is listening. God wants nothing but the best for you and wants you to expect the same.

January 9th

Your Inheritance is Priceless

If you were told that you had a $10 million inheritance coming to you, would you accept it freely? I know that I would!

We all have an inheritance that is worth so much more than any amount of money, but there are many who refuse to accept it. Will you accept your priceless inheritance?

The Bible tells us in Romans 8:16-17(NASB): *"The Spirit Himself testifies with our spirit that we are children of God, and if children, heirs also, heirs of God and fellow heirs with Christ, if indeed we suffer with Him so that we may also be glorified with Him."*

The way to receive this inheritance is simple, accept Jesus, the son of God, into your heart by accepting that He died for your sins on the cross, rose again and is seated in heaven with God the Father.

January 10th

Faith & Fear

Allowing fear and anxiety to enter your thoughts suffocates Faith. Many very real things occur that make us anxious or cause fear. Just look around or read the news headlines.

I have battled anxiety for most of my life and noticed an amazing change once I devoted my time to my faith and prayer. By reading and learning about how God cares for me, I've been able to overcome my fears and anxiety. My faith is drowning my fears.

The Bibles says in 1 Peter 5:7 (NASB): *"Cast all your anxiety on Him, because He cares for you."*

Allow God to take your fear and anxiety away and replace it with Faith.

Tuned In

When fine tuning a car radio, there is a sweet spot that will give the clearest signal. As you drive away from the strong signal, interference begins and, ultimately, the signal is lost.

Our lives and the Holy Spirit are very similar. When we are close to God and living in the Spirit the signal is very clear. As we move away, we encounter interference…outside distractions. If we travel too far away from God, we can lose the signal.

The Bible says in Galatians 5:25 (NASB): *"If we live by the Spirit, let us also walk by the Spirit."*

Make a point this day to move closer to God and be in tune with the Holy Spirit.

January 12th

Training Tools

A simple Google search yields results for every type of training, whether it be training an animal, a child, an employee or one's self. With any kind of training, there needs to be a foundation and a continual exercising of the principles taught.

Athletes who excel at a given sport usually dedicate a great deal of time to improving in those areas that help them perform at a high level. While some athletes are gifted with skills, they still need to study, exercise and practice to become better.

One training guide not included in a Google search is the Bible. God gave us a wonderful instruction manual to follow!

The Bible tells us in Proverbs 22:6 (NASB): *"Train up a child in the way he should go, even when he is old, he will not depart from it."*

I encourage you to use the Bible as a tool to strengthen your mind, body and soul.

January 13th

Building Up or Tearing Down

It's common to see people tearing each other down on social media, in the political arena, at school and even within families. This practice is the complete opposite from how God intends us to act towards others.

Ephesians 4:29 (ESV) says: *"Let no corrupting talk come out of your mouths, but only such as is good for building up, as fits the occasion, that it may give grace to those who hear."*

Do your part to build others up and make this world we share a better place.

January 14th

God's Strength

On my first international mission trip to Kenya, I was asked share words of encouragement to people living with disabilities.

Before speaking, I prayed that God would work in and through me to bring the people a message they needed to hear. I remember reading about Nick Vujicic, who was born with no arms or legs. As a teenager, Nick considered suicide, but received Christ instead. Nick is an evangelist today and is married with two kids. I shared Nick's story to encourage the Kenyans.

God wanted the people to see He can and will use them and their talents. God wants them to focus on the abilities He gave them. God wants the same for each and everyone one of us as well.

In closing, I shared the verse from Philippians chapter 4 verse 13 (NLV): *"For I can do everything through Christ, who gives me strength."*

Rely on God's strength to meet your own personal challenges and struggles.

January 15th

Prayer of the Week

Psalm 105:1 (NLT)

"Give thanks to the Lord and proclaim His greatness. Let the whole world know what He has done."

Pray to God to allow the Holy Spirit to work in and through you so that the non-believing world will see His glory in your daily life. Give thanks to Him always and in all ways.

January 16th

Choose Growth

Life is full of various trials – some are repeated. I have learned many valuable lessons from my life's struggles, most notably three job losses over the past decade. The first job loss produced some growth but left me wondering why it happened to me. The second time, I had a better outlook on the future and saw God there. After the third loss, I chose to have joy. Knowing God was with me through it all gave me great security.

This testing has brought tremendous growth in me spiritually, mentally and emotionally. Although I am not done growing, I am maturing in my faith and reliance on the one true God that loves me and protects me in all ways, always!

James 1:2-4 (NLT) says: *"Dear brothers and sisters, when troubles of any kind come your way, consider it an opportunity for great joy. For you know that when your faith is tested, your endurance has a chance to grow. So, let it grow, for when your endurance is fully developed, you will be perfect and complete, needing nothing."*

No matter what your current situation or trials, know that God is with you and is assisting you in your growth. God wants you to learn a valuable lesson. Will you be receptive to His teaching and choose joy?

Manage Your Time Wisely

According to people spend most of their waking hours (2018), the average American spends more than 11 hours per day interacting with media. That adds up to 167 days or 45% of the year.

Jones (2013) says the average American gets an average of 6.8 hours of sleep a night. The amount of time left in the day after sleeping and interacting with media is roughly 6 hours. Time spent working (2015) states the average American works just over 8 hours a day.

The above numbers are more than the time in a day! Today much of the data we receive is from an electronic device – I researched and wrote this devotional with a laptop computer. I read *Our Daily Bread* every morning using my smart phone.

Where do you fall on these averages? What are you doing with your time interacting with media? Are you learning, growing and becoming wiser?

In Psalm 90:12 (NASB) the Bible says: *"So teach us to number our days, that we may present to You a heart of wisdom."*

God wants us to use our time here on Earth for good. Make every day meaningful.

January 18th

Love People

Vehicles, televisions and other objects serve a purpose in this world. Objects are not meant to be loved; they are meant to be used. People were created by God to be loved, but over time this principle has been corrupted.

Christian writer Warren W. Wiersbe said, "In our universe there is God and there are people and things. We were made so that we should worship God, love people and use things. However, if we worship ourselves, we will ignore God, start loving things and begin to use people."

The Bible says in Galatians 5:14 (NASB): *"For the whole Law is fulfilled in one word, in the statement, "You Shall Love Your Neighbor as Yourself."*

Let the people in your life know that they are loved and more important than any object could ever be.

What Are You Chasing?

Society emphasizes all our nice possessions. Who looks the best and what designer they are wearing? What brand and year is the vehicle in the garage? How lavish is the home? The list goes on.

I recently read an article about a young man who sold a kidney to purchase an expensive phone and is now bedridden for the rest of his life. My wife told me she heard that people were selling personal belongings and taking out loans to buy Christmas gifts.

The bible says in Ecclesiastes 6:9 (NLT): *"Enjoy what you have rather than desiring what you don't have. Just dreaming about nice things is meaningless – like chasing the wind."*

If you or someone you know struggles with these temptations, lift them up in prayer to be released from chasing after the wind and that God will place in their heart a more meaningful pursuit.

January 20th

Big Adventure

Life is full of wonderful things, but we become too busy to realize what is before us. Children see small things and realize greatness. We can all learn from children if we slow down long enough to listen and learn from them.

I like to take my son on adventures. An adventure can be a trip to the store, a walk on the bike path near our home or an all-day excursion to hike at a state park. My son calls them big adventures with Daddy. We eagerly explore the things we encounter along our way. It gives me great joy to see how my son views creation and its splendor.

The Bible says in Matthew 18:3 (NASB): *"And said, 'Truly I say to you, unless you are converted and become like children, you will not enter the kingdom of heaven.'"*

Remember when you were a child and the way you viewed all things. Allow that awe and wonder be rekindled in your heart.

January 21st

Forecast

There are forecasts and predictions made for interest rates, stocks, weather (blizzards, tornadoes, hurricanes, flooding), volcanic activity, earthquakes, tsunamis and outcomes of sporting events. Dictionary.com defines forecast as, "to predict (a future condition or occurrence); calculate in advance."

Throughout the Bible, prophets made predictions about the future with great accuracy. Prophet is defined as, "a person who speaks for God or a deity or divine inspiration." (Dictionary.com) Moses predicted the Messiah in Deuteronomy 18:15 (NIV): *"The Lord your God will raise up for you a prophet like me from among you, from your fellow Israelites. You must listen to Him;"* and in the parallel passage of Acts 3:22 (NIV): *"For Moses said, 'The Lord your God will raise up for you a prophet like me from among your own people; you must listen to everything He tells you.'"*

Forecasters and prophets predict future events, but the prophet does so with guidance received from God. Revelation 1:8 (NIV) says: *"I am the Alpha and the Omega,"* says the Lord God, *"who is, and who was, and who is to come, the Almighty."*

January 22nd

Prayer of the Week

John 17:15(NIV): *"My prayer is not that you take them out of the world but that you protect them from the evil one."*

Jesus wants us to be protected from evil and from Satan. Attacks will come and you need the power of God in you corner. Pray for protection from God to surround you all the days of your life.

January 23rd

Love for All

The highest form of love, charity and "the love of God for man and of man for God" as defined on Wikipedia.org of the ancient Greek word.

In Matthew 22:37 (NASB), Jesus said: *"You shall love your Lord with all your heart, and with all your soul, and with all your mind."*

There are many different forms of love, for a spouse, for other family members and for friends.

Make a point today and every day to share love with everyone in your life.

January 24th

Striving for Perfection

I wake up each day and strive for perfection. I want to be the perfect husband, father, brother, son and servant to God. At some point, I always fall short.

During sporting events the players also try to have the perfect game, especially during the playoffs. The referees want to do their best and have the perfect game, but often come under scrutiny when they miss a call, especially one that may determine the outcome.

During the entire game there are numerous mistakes made by players, coaches and, yes, the referees. Each player, coach and referee are out there trying to do the best that they can with the skills they have been given by God.

No matter how hard anyone strives for perfection we will not achieve it. The Bible tells us in Hebrews 13:8 (NLT): *"Jesus Christ is the same yesterday, today, and forever."*

Make it a point to be forgiving of ourselves and others; we are only human.

Your Life is Priceless

The value of human life in economic terms has been calculated by various countries and in the United States by several different government organizations.

According to Value of life (n.d.) Australia has the value set at $4.2 million as of 2014, New Zealand has set the value of life at $3.85 million as of 2013 by the Treasury, Russia has different values ranging from $40,000 up to $2 million, U.S. Environmental Protection Agency has set the value of life at $9.1 million as of 2010, The Food and Drug Administration says the value is $7.9 million as of 2010, and the Department of Transportation has the value at $9.6 million as of August 2016. But none of these statistics matter to our Creator. God wants you to know that you are invaluable. In John 3:16 (NASB) Jesus says: *"For God so loved the world, that He gave His only Son, that whoever believes in Him shall not perish, but have eternal life."*

No matter where you are in life or what kind of problems you face, you are known, loved and cared for by God. Take the step today pray for someone you know to hear this message and receive salvation. If you need to pray this prayer to receive salvation, ask God for forgiveness of your sins, accept that Jesus lived, died and rose again to forgive those sins and conquered death; accepting that Jesus is your Lord and Savior. Amen.

January 26th

Pray

It doesn't take long to find out how people feel about politics when skimming social media or watching the news. People state how they feel and if they are met with opposition, they begin attacking. We are all made differently and should be treated with respect. Differing opinions should be respected.

When I was growing up, we were told that if you have nothing nice to say then don't say anything at all. The world would be a better place if adults would respect one another and accept differing viewpoints. We should be good examples for our children. We all share the same planet, why not make it a better place?

The Bible says in 1 Timothy 2:1-2 (NLT): *"I urge you, first of all, to pray for all people. Ask God to help them; intercede on their behalf and give thanks for them. Pray this way for kings and all who are in authority so that we can live peaceful and quiet lives marked by godliness and dignity."*

The next time you feel the need to prey on someone, pray for them instead. Praying can and has and will continue to change the world for the better.

You're Beautiful

According to Global cosmetic products (2018), the global cosmetic market was valued at over $532 billion U.S. dollars in 2017. By 2023, the market with be worth an estimated $805 billion U.S. dollars.

Society puts much emphasis on looking a certain way. Celebrities and models are idolized. There are even apps to enhance or filter images. I sometimes don't recognize people in public because they look nothing like the photos I see on social media.

Men and women are competing for mates and looking for certain characteristics that stand out to them – beauty plays a major role. But beauty is so much more than what a man or woman looks like on the outside. The heart of a person is what is important.

Proverbs 31:30 (NASB) says: *"Charm is deceitful, and beauty is vain, but a woman who fears the Lord, shall be praised."*

Know that you are beautiful, just the way God made you, inside and out. Let your beauty shine for the whole world to see.

January 28th

Τετέλεσται (It is finished)

Sin nature is choosing our free will over the will of God. We all have an inherent ability to want to rebel against authority. I have rebelled so much that I thought God wouldn't want me anymore and I would be unable to overcome my sin nature in areas that had a strong grip on me. I was wrong in my thinking.

In my 20s as I struggled to identify who I was, I became prey to nicotine. As a college athlete, I knew better than to use tobacco, but my body craved it. I used tobacco for nearly eight years before finally quitting. When I speak to people about this addiction, I tell them it was the worst habit to start and the best one to quit – 14 years now!

When we are in the middle of the war, it seems so hard to break loose, but once we do it brings so much freedom.

The Bible says in John 19:30 (NASB): *"Therefore when Jesus had received the sour wine, He said, 'It is finished!' And He bowed His head and gave up His spirit."* Τετέλεσται is the Greek word used meaning "It is finished!"

Know that Jesus has already won the battle for you and can help you overcome your sins!

Prayer of the Week

Psalm 17:6(NIV)

"I call on you, my God, for you will answer me; turn your ear to me and hear my prayer."

You have a direct hotline to God that is available 24/7. Call upon the name of the Lord when you pray knowing that he will pick up.

The Way of the World

I recently was in the market for a used truck. The salespeople I trust didn't have any suitable vehicles. I extended my search to dealers beyond my comfort zone. My search yielded a large amount of results, so I narrowed the field to a few to test drive.

At one lot, I test drove a truck and had my mechanic inspect the condition of the vehicle. The vehicle had an issue with the engine that may be costly to fix. After taking the vehicle back to the dealer, I discussed the issue and how it could be resolved. The salesmen told me something to the effect that you don't know what you get when buying a used car. He also told me, "It's just the way of the world." I thanked him for his time and left the lot.

The Bible says in Romans 12:2 (ESV): *"Do not be conformed to this world, but be transformed by the renewal of your mind, that by testing you may discern what is the will of God, what is good and acceptable and perfect."*

Stay close to God and His teaching so when you are in a situation needing clarity, you will find it and know without a doubt you are in His will.

January 31st

28 Days

New Year's resolutions have four weeks to become new habits. Habits, whether good or bad, can begin or end in this short amount of time. Depending how ingrained a habit is, it may take much longer to break than to start.

There are many habits or even addictions that are not good for us. Drugs, pornography, alcohol and tobacco are not good for us. Overuse of electronic devices, television or video games can be bad too. The good news is that these strongholds can be broken and replaced with new, good habits.

In Colossians 3:9-10(NASB) the Bible says: *"Do not lie to one another, since you have laid aside the old self with its evil practices, and have put on the new self who is being renewed to a true knowledge according to the image of the One who created him."*

Even though we are four weeks into the new year, today can be day one to stop a bad habit or start a new, good one. A good one to start would be reading the Bible or a daily devotional. Pray that God will help you put away the old habits and make room for the new ones!

February

February 1st

Where does your help come from?

Most people have a few close friends or relatives that they can count on to assist when in times of need. Support comes in the form of a helping hand, an ear to listen or a word of advice.

In the book of Job, God allowed Satan to afflict Job with many calamities. Job's friends tried to help him with their own insights. Neither Job nor his friends knew that God had allowed these things to happen. God wanted Job to completely rely on Him.

It is good to have support from friends and family. It is great to have guidance from our heavenly Father! In Psalm 121:2 (NIV) the Bible states: *"My help comes from the Lord, the Maker of heaven and earth."*

Allow the Lord to be your great adviser when you need help!

February 2nd

One Goal

Most people, if not all, have been assigned a single task to complete at some point in their existence. Some succeed while others fail. I have failed miserably at different points in my life, while succeeding greatly in others.

My life consists of many things that I want to accomplish. I can complete many tasks for an employer or a list of chores at home. But I have grown in my faith I now understand that there is one command that I am to do as a Christian.

The resurrected Jesus said in verse 19 of Matthew chapter 28 (NASB): *"Go therefore and make disciples of all the nations, baptizing them in the name of the Father and the Son and the Holy Spirit."*

We Christians have the amazing opportunity to share the love of Christ with everyone. Make a point to be bold and share the gospel with all you encounter from this day forward.

February 3rd

Bitter Cold

North America has seen record lows with wind chill lows of -50F (-45). At these temps, the body diverts blood supply to keep the vital organs warm and well. The extremities suffer as a result.

It's like our relationship with God. The more sin we have, the further from God we are where it is cold. At the core we are still alive in Him, but the rest of our body is suffering.

In Matthew 24:12 (NLT) Jesus says: *"Sin will be rampant everywhere, and the love of many will grow cold."* God desires a strong relationship with you and where there is closeness, there is warmth and love.

Draw near to the Lord who can keep you close and provide you with loving-kindness.

The End

I once read a book about living as if you only had one month left on this side of eternity. This book helped me overcome my fears and start truly living. The time I wasted on mundane activities came to an abrupt stop and I started to focus on the things that really matter.

The truth is that if you are alive today, you will see an end to this life. Some who read this may not be here a year from now. Chances are you know someone that has passed away recently. Approximately 250 people die every minute throughout the world from various causes. Death does not discriminate.

There is good news. Ecclesiastes 3:2 (NASB) says: *"A time to give birth and a time to die."* By accepting Christ as your personal Lord and Savior, you can be reborn into the family and spend eternity with Him.

Take the steps now to start living your life fully and with eternity in mind.

Prayer of the Week

Luke 6:12 (NIV)

"One of those days, Jesus went out to a mountainside to pray, and spent the night praying to God."

Jesus, the son of God, needed to communicate with His Father for an entire night. Maybe you have a lot to say to God and need to set aside time to lay it all out for Him.

Pray for time to get alone with God for an extended period this week.

February 6th

Amen

Most people have heard and even said amen at one point or another during their lifetime. I did some digging to find where the word comes from.

The definition of Amen is: "It is so; so be it" (used after a prayer, creed or other formal statement to express solemn ratification or agreement). Amen (n.d.) is derived from the Hebrew verb that means "to believe."

The Jewish, Christian and Muslim religions use amen as a concluding word at the end of prayers, according to wikipedia.org.

In 1 Chronicles 16:36 (NASB) the bible states: "Blessed be the Lord, the God of Israel, from everlasting even to everlasting. Then all the people said, 'Amen,' and praised the Lord."

Now you know when, where and why the word is spoken. Can I get and amen to that?

February 7th

What If?

Businesses entities, groups and individuals ponder this question when looking back at the past and in preparation for the future. Contemplating can help one decide the best direction possible with the information at hand.

I like to make contingencies for just about every situation. While this is a good quality to an extent, I have learned to keep this question in perspective. My family time used to be affected by me constantly running 'what if' scenarios. If this is something you struggle with, find a happy medium so you don't miss out on present joy. Now I take my what ifs to God in prayer.

In 1 John 5:14 (NASB) the Bible says: *"This is the confidence we have in approaching God: that if we ask anything according to His will, He hears us."*

Go to God in prayer with confidence so he can answer your questions.

February 8th

Patience

We have all struggled with patience at one point. When we try to push an agenda and are unable to move forward, we become impatient.

Psalms 27:14 (NASB) the Bible says, *"Wait for the Lord; Be strong and let your heart take courage; Yes, wait for the Lord."*

Next time you find yourself in this situation, look to the Lord and remember He has reasons for you to be patient. God just might have something better for you than you could ever imagine.

February 9th

Intentions

We all view interactions with people through different lenses. Through our culture, beliefs and past experiences, we form perceptions. Those perceptions become our reality. For instance, I cringe when a certain tone is reached in a conversation because my perception is that I have done something wrong and now it is time to pay the price. Then I stop, think about the situation and realize that the conversation is usually with someone who loves me. Because of the tone from past experiences, I used to believe history is repeating itself.

Discernment will help you to know the difference. Someone who loves and cares for you isn't out to hurt your feelings or upset you. However, there are people who may be out to inflict emotional distress.

The Bible says in 1 Corinthians 16:14(ESV): *"Let all that you do be done in love."* Keep this verse close to your heart in your conversations. Are you saying something with love? Is someone telling you something in love?

Pray for God to give you a heart that will know the difference between someone who loves you and one that is out to harm you.

The Fog

The Golden Gate Bridge in San Francisco, CA, is a majestic marvel that towers above the water almost 750 feet. However, a layer of dense fog often makes the bridge disappear. There are times in our lives when we are surrounded by dense fog and don't seem to be able to see God.

The Bible even tells us in 1 Corinthians 13:12 (THE MESSAGE): *"We don't see things clearly. We're squinting in a fog, peering through a mist. But it won't be long before the weather clears, and the sun shines bright! We'll see it all then, see it all as clearly as God sees us, knowing him directly just as he knows us!"*

Know that God is always there for you even when you are unable to see Him. We will see Him in all His glory once the fog lifts and the sun shines!

February 11th

Reborn

Babies are born into a world of sin. There is hope for all who are born into this world, despite being born into sin.

That day came for me on July 27, 2000. I was reborn, my second birth by accepting that Jesus lived a sinless life, died on the cross for my sins and has risen and now sits at the right hand of God in heaven.

There have been struggles along the way after being baptized into the family, but growth during those times has made me learn and continue to press in on God. The Bible tells us in 2nd Corinthians 5:17 (NLT): *"This means that anyone who belongs to Christ has become a new person. The old life is gone; a new life has begun!"*

Have you been reborn? If so, start celebrating it with your friends and family. If you have yet to be reborn, you're welcome to join the family!

February 12th

Prayer of the Week

Romans 8:26 (NIV)

"In the same way, the Spirit helps us in our weakness. We do not know what we ought to pray for, but the Spirit himself intercedes for us through wordless groans."

Prayer doesn't always make sense to the person praying, but it does to God. Pray even when you don't know how to say what is in your heart or on your mind.

Forgiveness

Matthew West's wonderful song "Forgiveness" is about something so simple and yet so hard for so many of us to do.

Here is a verse from the song:
"It'll clear the bitterness away,
It can even set a prisoner free,
There is no end to what its power can do,
So let it go and be amazed by what you see through eyes of grace.
The prisoner that it really frees is you,
Forgiveness, forgiveness,
Forgiveness, forgiveness."

Is there someone you are struggling to forgive – or yourself? I had a time forgiving myself for things I have said and done over the years. With a greater understanding of God's grace and mercy, I have been able to forgive others, as well as myself.

The (ESV) Bible says in Ephesians 1:7: *"In Him we have redemption through His blood, the forgiveness of our trespasses, according to the riches of His grace."*

Take the time today to forgive someone or yourself. It will set you free!

February 14th

Valentine's Day

Americans usually open their wallets to spend $30 billion on Valentine's Day – that's a lot of cards, chocolate, flowers, and jewelry. Let's look at what the Bible says about love in 1 Corinthians 13:4-7 (NIV): *"Love is patient, love is kind. It does not envy, it does not boast, it is not proud. It does not dishonor others, it is not self-seeking, it is not easily angered, it keeps no record of wrongs. Love does not delight in evil but rejoices with the truth. It always protects, always trusts, always hopes, always perseveres."*

How you ever heard of the 5 Love Languages® - The Secrets to Love that Lasts by Gary Chapman? Check out the website (5lovelanguages.com), take the quiz and show that special person how much you care by learning their love language and speaking it to them every day!

February 15th

God with Us

No matter what life's circumstances are for you at this moment in time, God is with you. It could be a job loss, a death in the family, a failed test, facing a bully or any other situation that has you unsettled. Rest assured…God is in the midst your troubles.

My pastor gave me a piece of paper with a verse on it when I found myself with high anxiety and stress. I now have this verse posted in my office.

2 Thessalonians 3:16 (NASB) states: *"Now may the Lord of peace Himself continually grant you peace in every circumstance. The Lord be with you all!"*

May God grant you peace now, today and forever! Amen.

February 16th

Selfie Society

With the digital age and cameras on nearly every device it is very easy to capture moments in time and share them with the world. Selfies (pictures taken of the person taking the picture) has become a part of the images taken. According to Cohen (2016) 93 million selfies are taken each day.

A brief internet search lead to a page with a list of selfie related injuries and deaths. The number of selfie accidental deaths between Oct. 2011 and Nov. 2017 259 deaths and 137 incidents that have been reported throughout the world (List of selfie-related injuries and deaths, n.d.).

Most of us have taken a selfie a one time or another. There is a real problem when someone is so enamored with themselves that they forget about others and their surroundings.

Jesus says in Mark 12:30 (ESV) Bible "'And you shall love the Lord your God with all your heart and with all your soul and with all your mind and with all your strength.'"

Pray that people will not fall into the trap of loving themselves more that they love God!

February 17th

Warning Signs

My wife and I recently spent a few days hiking near our home in Ohio. We sought out trails for some adventure and to enjoy God's beautiful creation. There were warning signs at most steep trails. Some trails had additional warnings due to ice on the rocks and paths from a snowstorm the previous week. Dangerous areas were closed. Despite the signs, there were fresh footprints of those who ignored the signs.

This reminds me of a time in my life when I ignored warning signs from God. God gives us warning signs during temptations toward a slippery slope.

1 Peter 5:8 (NASB) says: *"Be of sober spirit, be on the alert. Your adversary, the devil, prowls around like a roaring lion, seeking someone to devour."*

Are there areas of your life where you see warning signs? Do you ignore these signs?

God's warning signs will prevent you from being harmed; don't ignore them.

February 18th

Listen

Hearing and listening are quite different. For instance, a man can hear his wife while watching a sporting event. A woman can hear her husband while she is making dinner. Each of these instances is an involuntary response to sound from the other person. In comparison, listening is intentional and takes focus on what is being heard.

A person can hear a sermon and not be listening to the lessons. You can read a book or this devotional and not be listening to the point being made. Our minds are filled with so many thoughts. It takes effort to clear all the clutter and concentrate.

The Bible says in Mark 4:9 (NASB): *"And He was saying, 'He who has ears to hear, let him hear.'"*

Do you hear, but not listen? Intentionally listen to God, loved ones, friends and strangers. We all want to be listened to, not just heard.

Prayer of the Week

James 1:6 (NASB)

"But he must ask in faith without any doubting, for the one who doubts is like surf of the sea, driven and tossed by the wind."

Pray each day this week with the full assurance that your faith is strong and able to withstand any storm you face. For even though you may be weak in faith, your God will give you strength.

February 20th

UnGODliness

The title of this devotional puts a central focus on God. Adding the additional letters creates a different focus and meaning to the root word God. Ungodliness means to deny or disobey God. Did God stand out to you? Did you have negative feelings when you read the title? Where you choose to focus, your heart follow.

Our daily focus distracts us to areas other than God, so we drift further from His plan for us. By removing the distractions that had nothing to do with God, it's easier to keep God as the central focus.

The Bible says in Colossians 3:2(NLT): *"Think about the things of heaven, not the things of earth."*

Take a moment to assess where your central focus is in daily routines and your walk with God. Is He at the center of all that you do? If not, refocus your efforts on God and see the changes He will bring.

February 21st

Paid in Full

After paying off a debt, the bank sent a letter marked "paid in full." What a great feeling to be free of a large debt!

How much greater would it be to have someone else pay a debt for you? Jesus did exactly that when He died for all mankind's sins on the cross.

In Luke 23:46 (NASB) the Bible says: *"And Jesus crying out with a loud voice, said, 'Father, into Your hands I commit My spirit.' Having said this, He breathed His last."*

My prayer for you is that you can know the wonderful feeling of understanding your debt of sin has been paid in full by Jesus Christ.

Thank God each day for allowing His son to pay the ultimate price for you!

February 22nd

Legacy

Legacy (n.d) is defined as a gift willed to someone – usually monetary. There is a much greater legacy Jesus wants us to enjoy.

Are you chasing worldly riches or are you putting work into the eternal kingdom? Many people work to make a name for themselves, but this life is about making the name of Jesus above all others.

In John 17:24 (NASB) Jesus says: *"Father, I desire that they also, whom you have given Me, be with Me where I am, so that they may see My glory which You have given Me, for You loved Me before the foundation of the world."*

Will your Legacy last through eternity? Take a moment to listen to John MacArthur's two-part sermon on gty.org titled "The Legacy of Jesus." This is a legacy worth building.

Role Models

Role model (n.d.) "a person whose behavior, example or success is or can be emulated by others, especially by young people." Most children look up to someone they want to be like. Do you remember your childhood role model and why you looked up to them?

Sometimes children don't realize their role model doesn't deserve their adoration. In my 20s, I wasn't a good model for anyone, but younger kids looked up at my successes and wanted to be like me.

Those whose examples I follow today all have one thing in common: they model their lives after Jesus Christ.

The Bible says in Matthew 16:24 (NASB): *"Then Jesus said to His disciples, 'If anyone wishes to come after Me, he must deny himself, and take up his cross and follow Me.'"*

February 24th

Impatience

Have you ever been stuck in traffic, waited anxiously for test results or lost patience with a young child? The traffic doesn't change, neither does the test results nor the child due to your lack of patience. The struggle within is greater than the situation itself.

We're all guilty of lacking patience. Then we mature and better understand what lack of patience produces – nothing good, just negative attitudes.

The Bible says in Proverbs 14:29 (NIV): *"Whoever is patient has great understanding, but one who is quick-tempered displays folly."*

Do you or someone you know struggle with impatience? Take a moment to pray for yourself and others to have more patience in all circumstances.

Rest

We live in a 24/7 society and work never seems to end. In the past, blue laws prohibited activities like shopping and banking on Sundays the day of rest.

Genesis chapter 2 verse 2-3 (NASB) says: *"By the seventh day God had finished the work He had been doing; so, on the seventh day He rested from all His work. Then God blessed the seventh day and made it holy, because on it He rested from all the work of creating that He had done."*

Take time to observe a day of rest from all your work each week.

February 26th

Prayer of the Week

John 15:16 (NASB)

"You did not choose me, but I chose you and appointed you so that you might go and bear fruit – fruit that will last – and so that whatever you ask in my name the Father will give you."

When you make your request to God in the name of Jesus, ask for things that are in accordance to the will of God because He will not honor those that are in direct conflict with His nature.

Choose to have Jesus as your most important role model so future generations can see how to live like Jesus.

Be Filled

Alcohol is a drug of abuse readily available at grocery stores, restaurants and convenience stores. In the United States there are also drive-through stores for purchasing beer and wine.

Growing up within my chosen circle of friends, it was easy to get alcohol. Alcohol lowers inhibitions and seems to make things more exciting. Looking back, most of my poor decisions were influenced by alcohol.

Today I choose to be filled with the Holy Spirit and my decisions are clearer and wiser.

The Bible says in Ephesians 5:18 (NIV): *"Do not get drunk on wine, which leads to debauchery. Instead, be filled with the Spirit."*

Do you struggle with alcohol abuse or know someone who does? Pray for that person to stop being filled with alcohol and start being filled with the Holy Spirit.

February 28th

Pointing Back at You

Have you ever heard about pointing a finger at someone and three are pointing back at you? In the world we live in today people use their thumbs on devices and thus have four fingers point back at them.

In John chapter eight the Pharisees were wanting to stone a woman for a sin she had committed. Jesus spoke to the Pharisees in John 8:7(NASB) concerning the woman, *"But when they persisted in asking Him, He straightened up, and said to them, 'He who is without sin among you, let him be the first to throw a stone at her.'"*

Instead of pointing out the sins of others, forgive them, love them and be a blessing to them. After all, we are all sinners and need forgiveness.

For February 29th see page 384

March

March 1st

Rotten at the Core

Many of us know someone who seemed to be living a healthy, Christ-centered life that bore fruit and, the next thing you know, they have somehow destroyed their life and or others around them.

In my living room recently drinking coffee while having my quiet time with God, I heard a loud crash and saw a tree fall. As this apparently healthy tree fell, it took out a few other branches from nearby trees. Upon further inspection, the tree was rotten at the core. The rotting process happened over time. The problem was at the heart of the tree with collateral damage to those surrounding it.

People can be fine by outward appearances, but rotten at the heart. When one falls, those closest can suffer damage too.

The Bible says in Proverbs 21:2 (NLT): *"Every way of a man is right in his own eyes, but the Lord weighs the heart."*

Is your heart or the heart of someone close to you filled with the love of Christ or empty and rotting? Take some time today to examine your own heart. Get to know the hearts of the people around you too. Damage to the heart can be repaired by God.

March 2nd

Justify

How many times have you reasoned with yourself about sin in your life? As a society, we want to reduce the weight of our sin in our own eyes. We say things like, "It's ok," "God made me this way," "It's not as bad as other sins I could be committing," or "I just can't help myself."

All sin is the same whether in thoughts, words or actions – it separates us from God. Let's end the debate about which sins carry more weight to justify our sins and accept them for what they are: sin.

The Bible says in Romans 6:23 (NASB): *"For the wages of sin is death, but the free gift of God is eternal life in Christ Jesus our Lord."* Sin is payable by death, yet we all have the right to the gift from God to eternal life.

Do you have sin that you have become desensitized to or need to accept God's gift? If you know God, confess and ask for forgiveness. If you need the gift, please pray this prayer right now: Lord, I am a sinner. I accept that Jesus lived, died and has risen for my sins so that I can be with you in eternity. I know in my heart that Jesus Christ is my Savior. I invite the Holy Spirit into my life to guide me on the path you have for me. I thank you and praise you in Jesus name I pray, Amen!

March 3rd

Leave an Open Chair

I recently sat down with a fellow Christian to have a business meeting over coffee. As we were discussing various matters, I pulled out a chair and commented that the seat was for God.

Looking back at my personal and business meetings throughout a nearly 20-year career, I can see a difference in those meetings where God had a seat.

In Matthew 18:20 (NASB) Jesus says: *"For where two or three are gathered in My name, I am there in their midst."*

Do you invite God to be part of your meetings when two or more are gathered? God wants to be present in all that you do. The next time and every time two are more are gathered, invite God to have a seat and feel the difference. You'll be glad you did.

March 4th

Prayer of the Week

Psalm 55:1 (NLT)

"Listen to my prayer, O God. Do not ignore my cry for help!"

It's ok to cry out to God and he expects you to desperately need Him. When praying this week, don't hold back your pleas to almighty God.

Conditions

Certain conditions need to be present for a plane to fly. For a tornado to happen, the atmosphere needs to be exact. For snow to fall instead of rain the temperatures need to reach 32 F (0 C). The list goes on and on.

Do you set terms on when you can interact with God? It's unnecessary, but most do. The list of reasons why we can't meet with God are endless: "I can't go to church because I am not dressed well enough." "God won't talk to me because I am not good enough.", "I have sin in my life and until I get rid it, God won't listen."

The Bible says in Romans 5:8 (NASB): *"But God demonstrates His own love toward us, in that while we were yet sinners, Christ died for us."*

God knows everything about you and He still loves you! The conditions are always right to cry out to God.

March 6th

Brevity of Life

Have you ever breathed onto a mirror and watched the fog dissipate almost immediately? Life is as short as that instance when viewed over time.

It's easy to get discouraged when thinking about the shortness of life. Consider changing your perspective! It can be a great encouragement to actively pursue meaningful relationships and focus on sharing the gospel of Jesus Christ.

The Bible says in James 4:14 (ESV): *"Yet you do not know what tomorrow will bring. What is your life? For you are a mist that appears for a little time and then vanishes."*

What can you start doing today to make a difference and spread the good news of Jesus Christ with those around you?

March 7th

Living Water

Clean water is a valuable resource to all of mankind. Our bodies are made mostly of water and to sustain life we need to drink it. In addition to consuming water, we use it to cook and clean. This Earth we share is comprised of more than 70% water.

Most Americans have water readily available at home. We don't think twice about it until the power goes out or a water well pump goes bad. In Africa, much time is spent each day finding a clean water source, retrieving it in jugs and transporting it to the home for use.

Jesus says in John 4:14 (NASB): *"But whoever drinks of water that I will give him shall never thirst; but the water that I will give him will become in him a well of water spring up to eternal life."*

No matter where or how you get your water, there is a source we can all easily obtain that brings eternal life. Will you accept water from the greatest well of all?

Do Not Call

Have you ever received a call about unpaid student loans or an expired vehicle warranty? I spend more time blocking numbers for spam than answering legitimate phone calls.

We all have someone or something that we need to block in our lives. Sin is a great example of something we should all strive to block.

What are you blocking in your life? God should not be blocked, but there are some people who add Him to the "Do Not Call" list when He calls upon them.

In John 12:48 (NIV) Jesus says: *"There is a judge for the one who rejects me and does not accept my words; the very words I have spoken will condemn them at the last day."*

Place God at the top of the "favorites" on your call list and answer when He calls you!

Indescribable

Have you ever received a gift that left you speechless with joy?

How do you show your gratitude for such a thoughtful gift? You say thank you or tell the person how gracious they are.

In 2 Corinthians 9:15 (NIV), the Bible says: *"Thanks be to God for His indescribable gift!"*

God gave each of us a gift that no words can describe. Take some time today to thank God for graciously giving the gift of salvation to all us who accept Jesus Christ as our personal savior. Pray for the lost who need to hear about this gift. Amen!

March 10th

Proverb Challenge

There is a challenge for just about anything today – some are good while others are not. Social media has popularized the not-so-good cinnamon challenge to see if someone can eat a spoon full of the spice, and the successful ice bucket challenge to raise money and awareness for ALS (amyotrophic lateral sclerosis).

However, there also is a life-changing challenge with eternal implications. The Book of Proverbs in the Bible is filled wisdom and instructions on living a Godly life.

Proverbs 1:7 (NLT) says: *"Fear of the Lord is the foundation of true knowledge, but fools despise wisdom and discipline."*

There are 31 chapters in the book of Proverbs. Read and study one chapter a day for the next 31 days to complete the Proverb Challenge. May God speak to you and guide you through this study.

March 11th

Prayer of the Week

Psalm 51:1 (NLT)

"Have mercy on me, o God, because of your unfailing love. Because of your great compassion, blot out the stain of my sins."

Make a point to regularly ask for forgiveness and cleansing of sins. Also, seek the help of the Spirit to not continue in the same pattern of sin.

Sharing the Light

Would you, having a light, not share the light with people stumbling around in darkness? I used to selfishly hide my light and conserve it so it would not go out. I misunderstood the purpose of my light.

Now I know to use my light to help others see. The people lost in the darkness have unlit torches ready but need someone with a burning torch to light theirs so they can help spread that light to others.

Jesus says in Matthew 5:14 (NLT): *"You are the light of the world – like a city on a hilltop that cannot be hidden."*

Make a point to seek out someone who is roaming in the darkness and light their torch with yours.

March 13th

Autopilot

Do you go to church, tithe, pray and repeat without thinking about it? If this sounds like your walk as a Christian, you are probably on autopilot.

This feature is being used in aircraft, ships, cars and even people. The idea is that the object will move without a person constantly at the controls, allowing said person to do other tasks. While caught up in other tasks the vessel can veer off course and potentially into a dangerous situation.

The Bible says in Hebrews 2:1 (NLT): *"So we must listen very carefully to the truth we have heard, or we may drift away from it."*

Take your vessel off autopilot to prevent yourself from drifting away from truth!

March 14th

Snow White

Have you ever watched snow falling from the heavens? For those who live in cooler regions, what a blessing to see this beautiful scene. Unfortunately, the brilliant, white, fluffy snow eventually becomes a nasty, brown, melted mess.

When we have sin in our lives, we are the dirty snow. Once the snow loses the original perfect form, it can never be restored. However, we can become as white as snow, according to the Bible.

In Isaiah 1:18 (NIV) the Bible says: *"'Come now, let us settle the matter,' says the Lord. 'Though your sins are like scarlet, they shall be as white a snow; though they are red as crimson, they shall be like wool.'"*

Jesus died for our sins and settled our debt for us. Even though we were once as the dirty snow, we are as clean as the freshly falling snow!

March 15th

What Are You Training For?

Some people spend massive amounts of time in the gym to build muscles and win competitions. Other people run long distances every day to compete in marathons. Men and women all over the world prepare for competitions to show off their skills among fellow athletes.

I used to train extensively for baseball, spending numerous hours practicing my hitting, running and throwing skills to be able to compete at the top level in hopes to stand out in the crowd and even get paid to play. Now I train for a different reason.

In the first letter from Paul to Timothy in Chapter four verse eight (NLT) the Bible says: *"'Physical training is good, but training for godliness is much better, promising benefits in this life and in the life to come.'"*

Start training your body today for the race to save souls tomorrow.

March 16th

Lent

Ash Wednesday is the start of Lent for Christians. Ever wondered what Lent was about or why it is celebrated by Christians around the world?

Jesus was baptized by John the Baptist, and in Matthew 3:17 (NASB) the Bible says: "...*and behold a voice out of the heavens said, 'This is My beloved Son, in whom I am well-pleased.'*"

Jesus was then called to the desert by Spirit where He was tempted by Satan. It was in those 40 days that Satan tempted Jesus to make bread out of stones, jump from high and angels would catch Him and worship Satan and in return Jesus could have all the kingdoms of the world (Matthew 4:1-11, NASB). Jesus defeated Satan and began his ministry after returning from the desert.

Many Christians throughout the world will fast or add devotions during Lent. What might you do this year for Lent in remembrance of Jesus' 40 days in the desert?

March 17th

Saints

This day is not all about drinking green beer or searching for a pot of gold at the end of a rainbow, chasing leprechauns or finding four-leaf clover.

St. Patrick's Day is a religious holiday celebrated on the day of death of this saint. St. Patrick was a missionary bringing his faith to the non-believers in Ireland. Some believe he used the three-leaf clover to explain the Trinity.

In 1 Corinthians 1:2 (NIV) the Bible says: *"To the church of God in Corinth, to those sanctified in Christ Jesus and called to be his holy people, together with all those everywhere who call on the name of our Lord Jesus Christ – their Lord and ours."*

We, who call on the name of the Lord, are saints. Let's thank Jesus today for laying his life down so that we can be holy. Amen!

March 18th

Prayer of the Week

1 Kings 8:23 (NIV)

"...and said: 'Lord, the God of Israel, there is no God like you in heaven above or on earth below – You who keep Your covenant of love with Your servants who continue wholeheartedly in Your way.'"

Solomon approached God with great reverence for how amazing He is. This week, practice opening in prayer for the magnificent Lord you serve and do it with all your heart and soul.

Attitude Adjustment

If you ever had a vehicle that was out of alignment, you know other problems occur as a result. The same thing can occur when a person's back is not aligned properly. A few adjustments in either case can bring a much smoother ride or stride.

From my mid-20s to mid-30s, I had an attitude that needed adjustment because I was angry about relationships and outcomes surrounding them. The angry attitude was replaced with an attitude of love and the outcomes improved.

In 1 John 4:16 (NLT) the Bible says: *"We know how much God loves us, and we have put our trust in his love. God is love, and all who live in love live in God, and God lives in them."*

A mechanic uses a machine to align a car; a chiropractor can properly align the back; and God can adjust a person's attitude.

Pray that God will adjust the attitudes that need to be realigned to one of love!

Forever

How long is forever? Ask a child and they may tell you it is next Friday when a new Pixar movie is released. Ask a young adult, and they may tell you next Tuesday when a new album or video game is released. Ask a Toyota owner and they may tell you it is 300,000 miles or when the body rusts out on their vehicle. Each of these people has a different perspective.

At different points in our lives, we have a different understanding of what forever means to us. All items listed will have an end, but time will continue. There is one thing that will and does last forever.

Psalm 107:1 (NIV) says: *"Give thanks to the Lord, for He is good; His love endures forever."*

Share this idea with someone who needs to hear that God loves them forever!

March 21st

SHMILY

Is it hard for you to see how much God loves you?
Could it be that you are looking too hard or are too
busy to take notice?

When I was in college, I was told about a way that a
husband and wife would show each other randomly
how they loved each other. The wife would hide a
'SHMILY" somewhere for the husband to find. Once
"SHMILY" was found, the husband would hide if for
the wife.

Psalm 68:19 (NLT) says: *"Praise the Lord; praise God our
Savior! For each day He carries us in His arms."*

God reveals Himself in many ways to each of us to "See
How Much I Love You." Where is God saying
"SHMILY" to you today?

The Wedding Ring

Have your heard that two months' salary is a good starting point to pay for an engagement ring or know why wedding rings are worn on the left fourth finger?

According to an article on Brides.com (https://www.brides.com/story/why-are-wedding-rings-worn-on-left-hand), "The importance of the circle. A circle has no beginning or end and is, therefore, a symbol of infinity. It is endless, eternal, just the way love should be. For many, the wedding ring is worn on the fourth finger of the left hand. This is because the vein in this finger was believed to lead directly to the wearer's heart."

The Bible says in Genesis 2:24 (NASB): *"For this reason, a man shall leave his father and his mother, and be joined to his wife; and they shall become one flesh."*

Showing your love by sharing vows and rings is an outward expression of the sacred bond of marriage. Love is in the heart, not just the ring on a finger.

March 23rd

Sharing the Truth

Would you share a cure for cancer or a new life-saving procedure with the world if you knew the answer? Most of us would say yes. Then why are we so slow to share the good news of the gospel that can save a person from an eternity apart from God?

I used to be afraid to speak about God to my own family, let alone complete strangers. God has taken me out of my comfort zone and is doing amazing things through me. My background is project management and business consulting, not writing. Nevertheless, God is using me in the way He desires.

The Bible says in Mark 16:15 (ESV): *"And He said to them, 'Go into all the world and proclaim the gospel to the whole creation.'"*

GIV365 already has subscribers from many countries – amazing! Please pray for God's hand over us, providing growth and guidance for the future of GIV365. Plant the seeds, God will make it grow!

March 24th

Be Specific

When receiving information about an item you would like to purchase, do you want the salesperson to be vague or do you want them to give you the most informative data? We all want the best description possible to make an informed decision.

Have you ever told someone that you would pray for them, then wonder in what areas they need prayer? Get as much useful information as possible so you can be specific in your prayer for them.

The Bible says in James 5:16 (NIV): *"Therefore, confess your sins to one another and pray for each other so that you may be healed. The prayer of a righteous person is powerful and effective."*

Healing may come with the specific prayer you lift to God!

March 25th

Prayer of the Week

Jeremiah 33:3 (NLT)

"Ask me and I will tell you remarkable secrets you do not know about things to come."

God told Jeremiah to ask Him for answers. When you ask God for answers, be prepared for what He will reveal to you that will help guide you in your daily walk.

March 26th

The Right Connection

Do you have trouble putting down your electronic devices and feel a need to be constantly connected? The technological world we live in today is difficult for many.

In our home, we have specific times when and where devices are prohibited. Too much screen time isn't good for the eyes and interactions with each other are more important.

The Bible says in Matthew 14:23 (NASB): *"After He had sent the crowds away, He went up to the mountain by Himself to pray; and when it was evening, He was there alone."*

Set aside time to disconnect from the world and allow yourself to become more connected with God.

March 27th

Overflowing Hope

Do you ever feel like you've lost hope? You're not alone. Look around a room and chances are others are also in despair. On the outside, they look like they have it all together, but on the inside, they are hurting. There is a cure.

Romans 15:13 (NIV) says: *"May the God of hope fill you with all the joy and peace as you trust in Him, so that you may overflow with hope by the power of the Holy Spirit."*

Pray that God will fill every person with the hope only He can give. Amen.

Fisherman

Are you a fisherman? A few may say yes. Are you a fisherman by trade? A smaller number would say yes. Are you a fisher of men? Every Christian should answer yes. Can you answer yes?

Matthew 4:19 (NASB) says: *"And He said to them, 'Follow Me and, and I will make you fishers of men.'"*

Jesus was very clear that if you follow Him, He would make you a fisher of men.

No matter how you earn a living, if you are a follower of Jesus, He will give you the skills to become a true fisherman.

My prayer is that you will learn to fish for the souls of those around you!

March 29th

A Season of Growth

Springtime in the northern hemisphere is welcomed with its warmer temperatures, birds chirping and blooming flowers.

The Bible says in Zechariah 10:1(NIV): *"Ask the Lord for rain in the springtime; it is the Lord who sends the thunderstorms. He gives showers of rain to all people, and plants of the field to everyone."*

Is there something you need to help you grow during this new season? Ask the Lord, the One who is the giver of all beautiful things.

Wants vs. Needs

My son insists that he needs Paw Patrol and chocolate. As a father, I explain to him that while he may desire to have certain items, he doesn't necessarily need them. The same is true for you and me.

As we get older, our wants become greater. The cartoon becomes a hit television series and the chocolate becomes an expensive steak from a high-end restaurant. The needs stay the same for the most part. We need oxygen, water, food, shelter and God.

In Psalm 23:1 (NLT) the Bible says: *"The Lord is my shepherd; I have all that I need."*

I am thankful for my God for His is good to me. Every need I have and then some is given to me by my Father in heaven.

Do you have everything that you need? Thank God for providing for your needs.

March 31st

Prayer of the Week

2 Chronicles 7:14 (ESV)

"If my people who are called by my name humble themselves and pray and seek my face and turn from their wicked ways, then I will hear from heaven, and I will forgive their sin and will heal their land."

God required then and still today for each one to pray in the same way. Forgiveness comes with a humble prayer, turning our back on the sin and running to God with a repentant heart.

April

April 1st

Don't Be Fooled

This is April Fool's Day, so watch out for fake news and unexpected pranks. Fool is defined as a person who lacks judgment or sense, according to dictionary.com

My wife and I played a prank on our social media a couple of years ago. We said, "There is a bun in the oven." This is a veiled hint at pregnancy. People congratulated us all day and that evening we posted a picture of a bread bun in our new oven – funny!

In Matthew 7:15 (NIV) Jesus says: *"Watch out for false prophets. They come to you in sheep's clothing, but inwardly they are ferocious wolves."*

May the spirit of God give you sound judgment every day. Amen!

April 2nd

April Showers

April rain in the United States ushers in renewed life to everything dormant from winter. Trees and flowers begin to grow and bloom and certain fungi like the morel mushroom begin to sprout up along the countryside.

Leviticus 26:4 (NASB) says: *"Then I shall give you rains in their season so that the land will yield its produce and the trees of the field will bear their fruit."*

Take a moment to look outside at what the wonderful rains from heaven are producing and give thanks to God!

April 3rd

Love Those Who Hate

One in 12 Christians (215 million) are being persecuted throughout the world (In a year, n.d.). It can be hard to fathom so many people being tormented because of their faith.

Americans are free to pursue God without fear of death. Our brothers and sisters around the globe are not always as fortunate. We hear stories about Christians who are praying for the people who want to harm them.

Jesus tells us in Matthew 5:44 (NIV): *"But I tell you, love your enemies and pray for those who persecute you."*

Please pray and love our enemies and those who are persecuting the family of Christians throughout the world in these dark and perilous times.

April 4th

Perfected

Quality standards are set forth for manufacturers of products throughout the world. Some have low standards of quality while others pursue perfection. Striving for perfection is honorable, but never obtained on this side of eternity.

We all have imperfections or sins that prevent us from being perfect. God created a way for us to be redeemed to a flawless state.

The Bibles says in 2 Corinthians 5:21 (NLT): *"For God made Christ, who never sinned, to be the offering for our sin so that we could be made right with God through Christ."*

Jesus made everything perfect by becoming sin in our place to redeem us to God! Take some time in prayer today to thank God for His gracious gift!

April 5th

World at Your Fingertips

According to Holst (2019), nearly 2.71 billion people have smartphones in 2019.

The world is more connected than ever before, but people feel empty. The ability to communicate via devices is increasing, while we struggle with real-life social interactions.

Technology opens doors for interactions across the globe. Through WhatsApp, I was able to video call my wife and son in Ohio while on a mission trip in Kenya. There is also a downside to the same technology. Smartphones have a variety of apps that can be addictive and distracting. There are so many sad stories about someone injured by a distracted driver using a smartphone.

Proverbs 4:25 (NASB) says: *"Let your eyes look directly ahead and let your gaze be fixed straight in front of you."*

Keep technology in its rightful place, as a tool, not a distraction. Focus on the Lord and all that He is doing in and around you.

April 6th

Cut Off

I recently purchased fresh cut roses for my wife on our anniversary. The flowers were very alive and vibrant. A week and a half later, they withered having been cut off from their source of life.

When we are close to God and receiving His nourishment, we are vibrant and alive in Him. If we are cut off from Him, it doesn't take long to fade.

Isaiah 40:8 (NASB) says: *"The grass withers, the flower fades, but the word of our God stands forever."*

No matter where you are in life, remember that staying close to God and His word will last longer than any season of your life.

April 7th

Just Passing Through

Business travel takes me to many cities throughout the United States, Canada and Africa as a temporary resident. Even though my time there is short, it is still my goal to have a positive influence on others.

This reminds me of 1 Chronicles 29:15 (NLT): *"We are here for only a moment, visitors and strangers in the land as ancestors were before us. Our days on earth are like a passing shadow, gone so soon without a trace."*

Do something to have a positive impact on those who surround you each day.

April 8th

Prayer of the Week

Ephesians 6:18 (NLT)

"Pray in the Spirit at all times and on every occasion. Stay alert and be persistent in your prayers for all believers everywhere."

This week take time to pray with the power of the Holy Spirit for your fellow believers around the world who are facing the same enemy as you.

April 9th

All In

Have you ever watched or played Texas Hold'em poker? Players buy in and receive a set amount of chips for betting. If a player feels they have a great hand, they may risk it all by going all in.

Part of my character is to go all in with certain aspects of life, whether it's sports or even Texas Hold'em. However, I always held back when it came to be giving myself to God.

In Matthew 22:37 (NASB) Jesus replies to a Pharisee: *"And He said to him, 'You shall love the Lord your God with all your heart, and with all your soul, and with all your mind.'"*

God wants us to be "all in" on our relationship with Him. Unlike the high-risk game of Texas Hold'em, we are guaranteed victory in Christ! Are you "all in?"

April 10th

Mindset

Do you live the way you want, pursue everything you need and then, if time is left, seek a relationship with God? This was my, once upon a time.

Jesus said in Matthew 6:33 (NLT): *"Seek the Kingdom of God above all else, and live righteously, and He will give you everything you need."*

Change your mindset and God will change your world.

April 11th

God's Calling

When God called you to follow Him, he did not say that you would be in first-class accommodations or tell you to get comfortable. If anything, He may have been saying: prepare yourself for a long, uphill climb with numerous twists and turns along the journey.

Creating videos for daily devotion is something new and make me uncomfortable – and that's the point. God wants us outside our comfort zone so we can grow.

Joshua 1:9 (NASB) says: *"Have I not commanded you? Be strong and courageous! Do not tremble or be dismayed, for the Lord your God is with you wherever you go."*

Remember, God is with you on the journey He has called you to.

April 12th

Broken Compass

Most people have either had or have been a friend with a questionable moral compass. There is hope for these persons, but it's a slippery slope leading to destructive behaviors.

Growing up and learning about Jesus provided me with a strong foundation to build my faith. When I stopped attending church, my compass lost its direction. Certain individuals I associated with began to reshape my morals. During this period of decline, my troubles began to mount. Looking back at that time in my life, I can now see clearly what had happened to me.

1 Corinthians 15:33 (NASB) says: *"Do not be deceived: 'Bad company corrupts good morals.'"*

Whether you are the bad influence or influenced by the bad, there is hope in Jesus for all. Trust in God and he will fix your compass and get you headed in the right direction.

April 13th

Freedom of Choice

Studies show adults make about 35,000 choices daily, which equates to 24 per minute. What guides your choices?

Looking back at my past decisions, I realize they didn't benefit me or anybody else. Now, my handbook – the Bible – guides me in making better choices.

Galatians 5:13 (NLT) says: *"For you have been called to live in freedom, my brothers and sisters. But don't use your freedom to satisfy your sinful nature. Instead, use your freedom to serve one another in love."*

Choose to serve others in love, rather than your former sin nature.

April 14th

Completing the Challenge

A little over a month ago you were given a challenge to read a chapter in Proverbs. Did you complete it?

2 Timothy 4:7 (NASB) says: *"I have fought the good fight, I have finished the course, I have kept the faith."*

The Proverbs challenge was designed to show you how easy it is to study the Bible daily and notice the changes that occur during that time.

My prayer is that you will apply the teachings in the Bible to your daily life and continue to grow in faith and love.

April 15th

Prayer of the Week

Jeremiah 29:12 (NIV)

"Then you will call on Me and come and pray to Me, and I will listen to you."

God doesn't have voicemail. He answers when you call. Start a new habit to have a call to God each day this week. He is waiting to hear from you and ready to listen.

April 16th

Relying on God

Do you think you are strong? Even when we feel strong enough to handle something alone, God can show how weak we are.

Relying on my own strength to conquer a battle in my mind often left me worse off after each attempt. When I gave up trying on my own, God's strength filled me in a way only He can. Our own strength takes us only so far. God's strength carries us farther than we can imagine.

2 Corinthians 12:10 (NLT) says: *"That's why I take pleasure in my weaknesses, and in the insults, hardships, persecutions, and troubles that I suffer for Christ. For when I am weak, then I am strong."*

Allow God's strength to get you through your present troubles.

April 17th

The Ultimate Sacrifice

Are you willing to sacrifice everything? Police, firefighters and members of the military routinely put their lives on the line to save others.

I train and serve with a band of brothers who know the risks we face each time we serve. We have each other's back should something happen during our watch. It is an amazing feeling to know that the guy standing next to you is willing to die to protect you.

John 15:13 (NLT) says: *"There is no greater love than to lay down one's life for one's friends."*

Pray for the men and women who put their lives on the line to protect us all from harm.

April 18th

Implement

Do you have faith in God? If so, do you allow your faith to show in the works you produce?

Many people proclaim their faith, but don't produce anything good. Implement the principles of the Bible into your life and you will produce goodness.

For example, a doctor goes to school for many years before practicing. If he or she doesn't apply their skills, they help no one and are therefore useless.

James 2:17 (NLT) says: *"So you see, faith by itself isn't enough. Unless it produces good deeds, it is dead and useless."*

Start implementing your faith into your life and see the good that it will produce.

April 19th

Need Rest?

Work, school, sports, friends, family, hobbies – there's always something to do and somewhere to be. We all need time to slow down and find relief from our burdens and blessings.

Matthew 11:28 (NIV) says: *"Come to Me, all who are weary and burdened, and I will give you rest."*

Our God wants us to come to Him and find rest in His presence. My prayer is that you will go to God and find the rest you need.

April 20th

Out of the Ashes

A giant sequoia tree needs fire for new growth to happen. The extreme heat from the fire allows the seed cones to open and release the seeds. The scorched earth allows the seeds to reach the soil and begin to grow (Yosemite sequoias need fire, n.d.).

John 12:24 (ESV) says: *"Truly, truly, I say to you, unless a grain of wheat falls into the earth and dies, it remains alone; but if it dies, it bears much fruit."*

Before you can grow, you must relinquish your old life. This can be done by accepting Jesus Christ as your personal savior. If you need to pray this prayer to receive salvation, ask God for the forgiveness of your sins, accept that Jesus lived, died and rose again to forgive those sins and conquered death; accepting that Jesus is your Lord and Savior. Amen.

April 21st

Stumbling Block

Are you talking but not walking? A quote from Brennan Manning provides perspective of what the non-believing world sees when this occurs.

"The greatest single cause of atheism in the world today is Christians who acknowledge Jesus with their lips, walk out the door, and deny Him by their lifestyle. That is what an unbelieving world simply finds unbelievable."

What a powerful statement – and one with which most of us can identify. How can we expect to reach a non-believer if we are not able to live out the faith?

James 1:22 (NIV) says: *"Do not merely listen to the word, and so deceive yourselves. Do what it says.*

Ask God to help you to absorb the word, then do what He wants you to do!

April 22nd

Prayer of the Week

James 5:13 (NASB)

"Is anyone among you suffering? Then he must pray. Is anyone cheerful? He is to sing praises."

Pray for all who are suffering with an illness, loss of job, loss of relative or friend, the effect of sin or any other ailments known to mankind. Also give thanks and sing praises to God for all the wonderful blessings He has given you.

April 23rd

SonRise

Each morning the sun rises in the east, also reminding us Jesus has risen. Some days we may not see the sun or feel the warmth, while other days it is shining bright and the heat is extreme.

The Bible says us in Psalm 73:28 (NIV): *"But as for me, it is good to be near God. I have made the Sovereign Lord my refuge; I will tell of all your deeds."*

Even though we feel distant from Jesus at times, He is always shining brightly.

April 24th

The Perfect Lawn

How much time and money do you spend on your lawn? Many people take pride in a green lawn free of dandelions and crabgrass but applying chemicals can rob the lawn of nutrients and several life forms.

The perfect lawn is full of life. Bees will come, pollinate plants, collect nectar and produce honey. The treated lawn may look good to the eye, but it is devoid of life.

Jesus says in John 10:10 (NLT): *"The thief's purpose is to steal and kill and destroy. My purpose is to give them a rich and satisfying life."*

Allow God to give you an abundant, meaningful life full of blessings.

April 25th

Rejoice

In the course of a day, you can face discouragement, loss and other adversity. Once the adversity arises you may become angry, hurt, bitter or anxious. How do you react? It's easy to rejoice when life is going well. When life isn't going great, it can be difficult to rejoice.

In 1 Thessalonians 5:16 (NASB) Paul says: *"Rejoice Always."* It does not say rejoice when you feel like it or only when things are going well.

My prayer for you today is that you will always rejoice in the Lord!

April 26th

He Carries You

"Footprints in the Sand" is a well-known story from an unknown author about how God carries His people. The story tells how a person is walking and sees two sets of footprints when life is going well, but only one when times are tough. The person asks why God wasn't present during those times and God replies it was during those times that He carried the person.

Isaiah 46:4 (NLT) says: *"I will be your God throughout your lifetime – until your hair is white with age. I made you, and I will care for you. I will carry you along and save you."*

Know that your loving God is carrying you when you need Him the most.

April 27th

The Path

Do you receive direction from God and then continue down your own path? If so, why? Is it because your trust in our own ways more than God's, do you think you have more insight into an issue than our omniscient God does or is it out of fear of the unknown? Or all the above?

God gave me the path He wanted for my life in 2012 and I listened, but only partially. A few years later, He spoke louder, and I listened a little more. And finally, in 2018, He made it so clear, that I listened and acted. I had a fear of the unknown and trusted my own ways more than His. God used those six years to prepare me for the day I allowed God's direction to be set into motion.

In Luke 11:28 (NIV) Jesus replied: *"Blessed rather are those who hear the word of God and obey it."*

Allow God to bless you by listening to Him and then being obedient.

April 28th

Encouragement

It has been nearly 17 months since GIV365 took root in my soul. The first year was dedicated to prayer and guidance from God. This year we reached a milestone with more than 100 devotionals completed.

I thank everyone praying for GIV365, affirming what God is doing and lifting us up with words of encouragement.

In 1 Thessalonians 5:11 (NIV) Paul says: *"Therefore encourage one another and build each other up, just as in fact you are doing."*

Let's pray that GIV365 will continue to encourage and be a blessing to those who are reached by the devotional.

April 29th

Prayer of the Week

Mark 14:36 (NIV)

"'Abba, Father,' He said, 'everything is possible for you. Take this cup from Me. Yet not what I will, but what you will.'"

Jesus provides a prime example of how we ought to pray. He made a request, but only if it was His Father's will. This week, practice praying for God's will – not your own – to be done in all matters.

April 30th

Palm Sunday

The week before Jesus rose from the grave, He made His triumphant entry into Jerusalem riding on a donkey. As Jesus traveled, people laid palm branches on the path He took. The Palm branch is a symbol of victory and peace.

The Bible says in Matthew 21:9 (NIV): *"The crowds that went ahead of Him and those that followed shouted, 'Hosanna to the Son of David!' 'Blessed is He who comes in the name of the Lord!' 'Hosanna in the highest heaven!'"*

Take time each year to give thanks to Jesus for making His fateful trip that would ultimately save the world!

May

May 1st

Battle Ready

Goliath was approximately 9 and a half feet tall and frightened many men. David was a young man and had skills that would defeat the mighty man with one sling of the stone with precision.

Who or what is your Goliath? Is it a boss, co-worker, the devil himself? Are you prepared to battle your Goliath? For me it was anxiety. I wasn't equipped to go to battle and kept finding myself defeated. Once I prepared myself, I finally found victory. My weapon is the word of God.

The Bible says in Hebrews 4:12 (NASB): *"For the word of God is living and active and sharper than any two-edged sword and piercing as far as the division of soul and spirit of both joints and marrow, and able to judge the intentions of the heart."*

Be filled with the word of God and the Holy Spirit in preparation for any Goliath you are facing.

May 2nd

30 Pieces of Silver

Nothing in this life is worth selling your soul – Judas Iscariot betrayed Jesus for the equivalent of one month's salary. Once Judas realized what he had done, he tried to give the money back, but in the end, he took his own life.

Jesus' fate was sealed with the kiss from Judas. The demise of Judas was that Satan entered his thoughts and overtook his heart.

Mark 8:37 (NASB) says: *"For what will a man give in exchange for his soul?"*

My prayer is that your heart and soul will always belong to God almighty!

Great Friday

Jesus faced a trial, was found guilty and sentenced to be crucified. Before his crucifixion, his jailors beat Jesus and gave him a crown of thorns. After this, He carried His cross to the hilltop and was nailed to it through His wrists and feet. The movie "The Passion of the Christ" does an extraordinary job showing the torture Jesus went through to save the world.

Luke 23:34 (NLT) says: *"Jesus said, 'Father, forgive them, for they don't know what they are doing.' And the soldiers gambled for His clothes by throwing dice."*

What a powerful example of forgiveness while being crucified. Jesus' love for mankind is pure.

Let's thank Jesus for bearing the sin of the entire world so we may have eternal life, amen!

May 4th

Peacefulness

Have you ever felt a sense of calm and peace before a storm? There is a quiet peacefulness that happens before the wind picks up and then skies open in a matter of minutes.

The storms of life can be the same, but most of the time we don't see a storm is on the horizon. Jesus knew His time had come, but the disciples probably felt a sense of peace after Jesus triumphant entry into Jerusalem.

Mark 4:38 (NLT) says: *"Jesus was sleeping at the back of the boat with his head on a cushion. The disciples woke him up, shouting, 'Teacher, don't you care that we're going to drown?'"*

When a storm arises, rely on the peace that comes from God!

May 5th

Communion

On the Eve of Jesus' crucifixion, He sat down with His disciples and had a last meal. Jesus knew what was going to happen and that He would be back at the right hand of His father in a short time.

Mark 14:22-24 (NASB) says: *"While they were eating, He took some bread, and after a blessing He broke it, and gave it to them, and said, 'Take it; this is My body.' And when He had taken a cup and given thanks, He gave it to them, and they all drank from it. And He said to them, 'This is My blood of the covenant, which is poured out for many.'"*

Remember Jesus and what He did for you.

May 6th

Prayer of the Week

Psalm 102:17 (NIV)

"He will respond to the prayer of the destitute; he will not despise their plea."

Pray for the poor and homeless this week. The world is full of hurting and less fortunate men, women and children, many who were displaced from war and are now refugees in foreign land.

May 7th

Now

Have you accepted Jesus as your personal savior? Now is the perfect time to accept Jesus, if you have not already done so. If you have, find a friend that could benefit from this life-changing experience.

John 3:3 (NIV) says: *"Jesus replied, 'Very truly I tell you, no one can see the kingdom of God unless they are born again.'"*

If you need to be reborn, pray this prayer. Lord, I am a sinner, I accept that Jesus lived, died and has risen for my sins so I can spend eternity with You. I know in my heart that Jesus Christ is my Savior. I invite the Holy Spirit into my life to guide me on the path You have for me. I thank you and praise you in Jesus name, amen!

May 8th

He Is Risen

On the third day, Jesus rose from the grave, conquering death and thus saving man from sin once and for all.

Matthew 28:6 (NLT) says: *"He isn't here! He is risen from the dead, just as He said would happen. Come see where His body was lying."*

May God continue to bless and protect each of His children throughout the world.

Believe

Thomas refused to believe that Jesus had interacted with the disciples until he saw for himself and placed his hand inside the wounds Jesus suffered on the cross. Air is something we do not see but gives life to all of us living. So too, Jesus gives us life even though we cannot see Him.

John 20:29 (NASB) says: *"Jesus said to him, 'Because you have seen Me have you believed? Blessed are they who did not see, and yet believed.'"*

You are blessed for trusting in the Lord whom you cannot physically see!

May 10th

Be Kind

Is it easy for you to be kind to your friends and family?
Most say yes. Is it easy to be kind to your enemies?
Most say no.

It is easy to show courtesy and grace to the ones we
love. Showing hate toward our enemies is an easy path
to take and feels natural because it is practiced so
regularly our society.

I once used the word hate and expressed that emotion
often enough that I became numb to the effects and the
true meaning of the word. The closer I grow to God, the
harder it is to go against His very nature of loving.

Proverbs 25:21 (NLT) says: *"If your enemies are hungry,
give them food to eat. If they are thirsty, give them water to
drink."*

Replace your anger and hostility toward your enemies
with love and compassion. The results will change you
and your enemies.

The Spirit

Prior to Jesus' ascension to heaven, He spoke to the disciples concerning the Holy Spirit.

In Luke 24:29 (NLT) the Bible says: *"And now I will send the Holy Spirit, just as my Father promised. But stay here in the city until the Holy Spirit comes and fills you with power from heaven."*

The Holy Spirit is within you as a believer; allow it to guide you in all things. You'll be glad you did.

May 12th

Never Bitter

Honey is sweet, while vinegar is bitter. The old saying is you can catch more flies with honey than with vinegar.

So too, when we speak to the non-believing world, we can reach them more easily with kind words and love versus judging and criticizing them.

Jesus says in John 15:17 (NASB): *"This I command you, that you love one another."*

If you have trouble reaching the non-believer, change your approach. After all, God is Love!

May 13th

Prayer of the Week

Romans 12:2 (NLT)

"Don't copy the behavior and customs of this world, but let God transform you into a new person by changing the way you think. Then you will learn to know God's will for you, which is good and pleasing and perfect."

Pray for a renewed filling of the Holy Spirit this week. Yield to the Spirit and allow your life to be centered around God for the rest of your life. Amen.

May 14th

Be Persistent

Do you ever feel you are on the course God has set forth, but the reward for your work is elusive? Continuing firmly in a course of action despite difficulty or opposition is the definition of persistence, according to dictionary.com.

2 Chronicles 15:7 (NLT) says: *"But as for you, be strong and courageous, for your work will be rewarded."*

Know that you will be rewarded at the right time by your Father in heaven if you stay the course.

The Dark Path

If you struggle with sin, this devotional is for you. The road to sin begins with a series of choices to go against God's will.

In 2 Samuel 11, David sins greatly. There were escape routes along the way, but David yielded to his lustful nature instead of pursuing the Godly answers. David first saw Bathsheba, then he sent for her to come to him and, finally, he committed adultery with her.

Proverbs 2:13 (NLT) says: *"These men turn from the right way to walk down dark paths."*

Use your free will to stay on the path God illuminates over the dark path that leads to destruction.

May 16th

Bullet Proof

I recently viewed a YouTube video of a team testing a ballistic shield that withstood multiple 40-caliber rounds, along with other munitions. It was a brilliant display of the strength of a man-made shield. How much greater is the One who protects us?

Psalm 28:7 (NLT) says: *"The Lord is my strength and shield. I trust Him with all my heart. He helps me, and my heart is filled with joy. I burst out in songs of joy."*

Let's sing songs of joy as we trust the amazing strength of our God and the shield with which He covers us.

May 17th

Seal of Approval

Have you ever cut a corner or not put in 100% toward work? You're not alone. Excuses vary for why work is subpar, such as being tired, or disliking an employer or fellow employee. It is time to stop making excuses and work diligently for your God.

The Bible says in Colossians 3:23 (NIV): *"Whatever you do, work with all your heart, as working for the Lord, not for human masters."*

Give God your best and He will take care of the rest.

May 18th

Be Happy

It is hard to enjoy life when you are anxious or worried about things that may arise in your life. I was recently listening to author Myron Golden on Latimer (2018), Myron said:

"Anxiety is never a good thing. Anxiety is caution over a future imagined danger. Anxiety is burning present energy on a future outcome that is undesirable to me."

Myron's statement hits home for me especially because I have battled anxiety all my life. Over the past year, I made a tremendous turnaround with the help of a verse in Philippians about giving it to God and focusing on the positive.

Philippians 4:6 (NLT) says: *"Don't worry about anything; instead, pray about everything. Tell God what you need and thank Him for all He has done."*

Take the energy wasted on anxiety and allow God to help you put it to good use!

The End of the Day

How does your day end? It often has to do with how it starts. Preparation at the beginning helps ensure it will end well.

I used to roll out of bed and go straight to work but wasn't prepared mentally to handle the day. This all changed when I made a point to spend the first hour or more of the day dedicated to my relationship with God. Now I have a much better understanding of how to handle difficult decisions because I am well prepared.

Proverbs 4:7 (NASB) says: *"The beginning of wisdom is: Acquire wisdom; And with all your acquiring, get understanding."*

Seek wisdom in the morning – it will carry you through the day.

May 20th

Prayer of the Week

Psalm 145:18 (NLT)

"The Lord is close to all who call on Him, yes, to all who call on Him in truth."

Pray to God with fully open and truthful dialog this week. God knows if you are being honest with Him and yourself. Keep God close by keeping it honest.

May 21st

Day of Prayer

The United States has a nation day of prayer at the beginning of May. You can have a day of prayer any day because it is a freedom granted to you by God.

Let's be united in prayer for God's guidance for our leaders, our people and our direction as a nation on a regular basis. We are the United States of America, not the Divided State of America.

The Bible says in 1 Thessalonians 5:17 (NASB): *"Pray without ceasing."*

Let us let the whole world know that we are still One Nation Under God!

May 22nd

Irons in the Fire

Do you ever feel you have too many commitments and not enough time to fulfill them? Leaving irons in the fire for too long will cause them to disintegrate, yet too short a time will make the iron difficult to shape it.

Business and personal relationships in life can be similar. Allowing relationships to sit too long may cause them to end. On the other hand, not warming up a relationship can make it difficult to mold it into anything substantial.

There is a third component to which we can all relate – with so many irons in the fire that it's hard to tend them all at regular intervals. The one being forged does well, while the others begin to suffer.

In Luke 10:41 (NIV) Jesus says: *"'Martha, Martha,' the Lord answered, 'you are worried and upset about many things.'"*

Focus on the important matters, unlike Martha, who was concerned about so many she forgot about the most important one: Jesus.

Balling

Are you balling? Balling is an adjective defined as possessing an abundance of money, possessions, property or other material goods; or used as a noun to describe an individual with well-rounded competence, significant affluence and physical prowess, according to urbandictionary.com.

A young man asked me what I do for a living and immediately followed it with, "You're Balling!" My response to the man was that I wouldn't consider myself as balling. I am just serving people the way I know how and doing it for the Lord. My bank account is not where my affluence comes from. It comes from the kingdom and God has blessed me with treasures surpassing any amount of money.

Jesus says in Matthew 6:21 (NASB): *"For where your treasure is there your heart will be also."*

Keep Balling for Jesus!

May 24th

Why Ask Why?

Do you ever ask why? Sometimes people spend so much time trying to figure out the why they miss the present moments in life.

I have wasted months trying to figure out why things happened around me, to me, to others...you get the point. As I grow closer to God, I realize that my comprehension of these matters should not be my focus.

The Bible says in Proverbs 20:24 (NLT): *"The Lord directs your steps, so why try to understand everything along the way?"*

Leave the why to God and be present in the moment.

May 25th

Memorial Day

Many people have cookouts and this day is the unwritten beginning of the summer party season. Graduations are happening, new adventures await a multitude during the summer months while school is not in session.

The last Monday in May each year is set aside to in America to honor and remember all who died while serving in the United States Armed Forces.

The Bible says in Psalm 147:3 (NLT): *"He heals the brokenhearted and bandages their wounds."*

Take some today between all the celebrating to remember those who died so we can enjoy our freedom. Have a safe and blessed day.

Character

Did you know your actions define your character? You may have the best intentions, but your actions tell the truth about you.

My wife and I attended an event recently where our son's behavior was on full display. You may think you know where this story goes, but not so quick! Our son gathered every person in the room and instructed them to hold hands in a circle, then lead them in prayer.

The Bible says in Proverbs 20:11 (ESV): *"Even a child makes himself known by his acts, by whether his conduct is pure and upright."*

Be vigilant that your actions are a clear indicator of your character.

May 27th

Prayer of the Week

Romans 12:12 (NIV)

"Be joyful in hope, patient in affliction, faithful in prayer."

Pray that you will be strong in your hope of the promise of Jesus Christ, have patience in dealing with all matters before you and remain devoted to seeking God's will in all that you do. Amen.

Fill in the Blank

Have you lost your passion or become complacent in your life? You are not alone. There are endless reasons why people lose their drive.

In a discussion with my wife recently, she let me know and the great enthusiasm for a project I'm working on didn't extend to her and our relationship. I became so focused on the project I was robbing my wife of her need to be loved and cherished.

The Bible says in Romans 12:11 (NLT): *"Never be lazy but work hard and serve the Lord enthusiastically."*

Take time to consider the areas in which you need to improve. Then fill in the blank with as many words you know need attention:

The Lord wants you to serve _____ with excitement. My prayer is you will have a renewed passion in the areas of your life where you have become complacent.

People Pleasing

Chances are you know or are a people pleaser. It is good to please people, but not to the extreme of feeling guilty or the exhaustion in trying to do so.

For the longest time, I tried to please everyone all the time. A couple of years ago, God showed me pleasing Him was much more valuable and required less effort. One reason is people's attitude and moods change like the wind.

Galatians 1:10 (ESV) says: *"For am I now seeking the approval of man, or of God? Or am I trying to please man? If I were still trying to please man, I would not be a servant of Christ."*

Seek God's approval in all that you do.

May 30th

Anger

"Enemies of the Heart" by Stanley (2011) says, "The root of anger is the perception that something has been taken. Something is owed you, and now a debt-to-debtor relationship has been established."

Look around and see why people are fighting. The politicians, the middle east, in your own neighborhood, even in your own family people are angry for these very reasons Andy talks about.

The Bible says in Ephesians 4:27 (NLT): *"For anger gives a foothold to the devil."*

Forgive the debtor's debt and be set free from anger. After all, Jesus released you and me.

May 31st

Magnificent Mondays

Many people dread Mondays because they're not happy at work. Perspective has everything to do with it.

As a small business owner, I enjoy the excitement of each day. For me, the first day of the week is Magnificent Monday when lunch hour means interacting with other Christian business leaders in a group called Impact Business Network. The group discusses life and business from a biblical perspective.

Psalm 133:1(NIV) says: *"How good and pleasant it is when God's people live together in unity!"*

I encourage you to change your perspective from the mundane to the magnificent.

June

June 1st

Success

How do you measure success? The world wants us to believe success means money, power, prestige. Some go to the extreme of obtaining such notoriety by illegal means.

In recent years, Ponzi schemes amassed billions of dollars for those at the top, while wrecking investors' personal finances. When you see someone else's wealth and accomplishments, it's not necessarily an indicator that of a blessing from God.

The Bible says in Psalm 37:7 (NLT): *"Be still in the presence of the Lord and wait patiently for Him to act. Don't worry about evil people who prosper or fret about their wicked schemes."*

May your accomplishments glorify God in all ways!

June 2nd

Mother's Day

If you're reading this, you have a mother to thank and celebrate! Whether your mother has passed on or you have a strained relationship – or things are great – be sure to thank your mother for giving you life.

The Bible says in Proverbs 31:28 (NLT): *"Her children stand and bless her. Her husband praises her."*

Take time each day to be thankful for your mother.

June 3rd

Prayer of the Week

Matthew 5:44 (NIV)

"But I tell you, love your enemies and pray for those who persecute you."

During your prayers this week, pour out love, forgiveness and kindness to those who are your enemies and who have hatred in their hearts. Love is a very powerful tool in fighting evil.

June 4th

Terrific Tuesdays

Have you ever woken up on a Tuesday and thought it would be a terrible day? A negative mindset sets the tone for the day.

I used to dread getting up and going to work, but now I start the day with a positive mindset, and it makes a tremendous difference.

Jeremiah 29:11 (NIV) says: *"'For I know the plans I have for you,' declares the Lord, 'plans to prosper you and not to harm you, plans to give you a hope and a future.'"*

Begin your day with God's plan and see how terrific it will be.

June 5th

Wondrous Wednesdays

Today is not Worrisome Wednesday, although many believe otherwise. Worry can affect anyone at any time and for any reason. Worry is the devil's way to undo God's plan for us. Time spent worrying is wasted when it could demonstrate our wonderful and faithful God.

Replace the weakness of worry by seeing God in everything. It's a life-changing experience to allow God to work in you.

Psalm 40:5 (NLT) says: *"O Lord my God, you have performed many wonders for us. Your plans for us are too numerous to list. You have no equal. If I tried to recite all your wonderful deeds, I would never come to the end of them."*

See and allow God's wonders to be present in your life.

June 6th

Tremendous Thursdays

The stress of the week often overcome us on Troublesome Thursday. If you have problems weighing you down, try adjusting your approach. Instead of seeing the problem, focus on finding creative solutions. Paul was imprisoned when writing to the Philippians. He spoke about how he was able to preach the gospel to the prisoners and guards. It would have been easy for Paul to become discouraged in his circumstances.

The Bible says in Philippians 1:13 (NASB): *"So that my imprisonment in the cause of Christ has become well known throughout the whole praetorian guard and to everyone else."*

Know and trust God to help you find solutions to all your troubles.

Super Sunday

Some people view Sunday as the end of the week and take the opportunity to party with friends the previous evening, resulting in a Sad Sunday. Others consider Sunday as the first day of the week devoted to seeing how super our God is to us. Changing your attitude about Sunday can do wonders for the mind, body and soul.

No matter how you view Sunday, one thing is certain: wherever you are in life, God has given you the greatest gift – salvation.

The Bible says in Ephesians 2:8 (NIV): *"For it is by grace you have been saved, through faith – and this is not from ourselves, it is the gift of God."*

Take time today and every day to gives thanks for our awesome God!

June 8th

Freedom Friday

Do you fear your deadlines won't be met or the date you have scheduled won't go as planned? Whatever is bothering you, the end of the work week is not meant to be Fearful Friday.

The Bible says in Psalm 34:4 (NIV): *"I prayed to the Lord, and He answered me. He freed me from all my fears."*

God wants you to have freedom from all your fears!

June 9th

Strong Saturday

Are you sick or have some sort of affliction that saps you of strength? This day is not Suffering Saturday. If you have some sort of ailment, focus on God and how He can carry you through.

Paul was given a thorn in the flesh, but he chose to see God, to rely on His strength instead of his present suffering.

The Bible says us in 2 Corinthians 12:9 (NASB): *"And He has said to me, 'My grace is sufficient for you, for power is perfected in weakness.' Most gladly, therefore, I will rather boast about my weaknesses, so that the power of Christ may dwell in me."*

God's strength can and will sustain you!

June 10th

Prayer of the Week

1 Thessalonians 5:17 (NASB)

"Pray without ceasing."

This week be in continual prayer keeping the lines of communication open to talk with God about everything, yes everything.

June 11th

Removing the Weeds

Have you ever seen a garden full of weeds producing good vegetables and vibrant flowers?

A major component of having a well-maintained garden is removing weeds. The weeds soak up the water, block out the sun and overtake the garden. It's critical to remove weeds on a regular basis.

Sin is like weeds in the garden. When we don't remove sin regularly from our lives, it destroys the good things we are trying to produce.

The Bible says in 1 John 1:9 (NASB): *"If we confess our sins, He is faithful and righteous to forgive us our sins and to cleanse us from all unrighteousness."*

When sin pops up in your life, be sure to weed it out quickly.

June 12th

GIV365

Today, like every day, is a blessing. The goal of GIV365 is to show how God Is Visible every day.

During my personal reading this morning during before the sun rose, I heard the birds chirping, saw the moisture on the blades of grass and felt the presence of God surrounding me with His love. You too can be immersed in His presence by making the commitment to do so.

The Bible says in Psalm 136:1 (NIV): *"Give thanks to the Lord, for He is good. His love endures forever."*

Please take a moment to give thanks to the Lord and share how God Is Visible in your life with those around you. Have a blessed day!

June 13th

There's No 'I' In Team

Championships are won by teams working together for a common goal. Even sports like golf are comprised of a team working with the golfer to play better.

Being a lone wolf only gets you so far. We were made to form partnerships with people and work together to achieve common goals. Be careful who you select for your team…there are those who are concerned only with their own status.

The Bible says in Ecclesiastes 4:9 (NLT): *"Two people are better off than one, for they can help each other succeed."*

Be a good teammate to your spouse, your co-workers and any other team you're on.

June 14th

Lust

Healthy sexual desire directed to one's spouse is encouraged throughout the Bible, specifically the Song of Solomon. When a person's desire is uncontrolled, it becomes lust. Left unchecked, these desires can lead to all sorts of sinful acts, as the Bible shows. The story of David and Bathsheba, for example.

The internet is a great resource, but it is also a tunnel that can lead to all sorts of sin. The statistics are staggering on how much time is spent in pornography on the internet. This addiction affects people from all walks of life.

The Bible says in Galatians 5:16 (NLT): *"So I say let the Holy Spirit guide your lives. Then you won't be doing what your sinful nature craves."*

Cling to the Holy Spirit for support and guidance in all areas of your life!

Gluttony

Gluttony (n.d.) is as a person who eats and drinks excessively. This sin also applies to selfish people. As a teenager, I remember not sharing candy and cookies with my family – I wanted what little I had all to myself.

The Bible says in Proverbs 11:25 (NIV): *"A generous person will prosper; whoever refreshes others will be refreshed."*

Learn to be generous with all that you have!

June 16th

Greed

Do you struggle with a strong desire to own nice things? You are not alone. This pursuit can become an obsession.

When you have a better understanding of God and His purpose, you realize life is about so much more than anything we can buy.

In Luke 12:15 (NLT) the Bible says: *"Then He said, 'Beware! Guard against every kind of greed. Life is not measured by how much you own.'"*

Make life about loving people, sharing the gospel and preparing for eternity.

June 17th

Prayer of the Week

James 4:3 (NLT)

"And even when you ask, you don't get it because your motives are all wrong – you want only what will give you pleasure."

Look at unanswered prayers and your motives this week. Practice praying according to God's will instead of your own.

Sloth

Most of us have encountered a lazy person who avoids working at all costs. Their effort reflects a lack of ambition.

American entrepreneur, author and motivational speaker Jim Rohn is quoted as saying, "Every life form seems to strive to its maximum except human beings. How tall will a tree grow? As tall as it possibly can. Human beings, on the other hand, have been given the dignity of choice. You can choose to be all, or you can choose to be less. Why not stretch up to the full measure of the challenge and see what all you can do (Jim rohn quotes, n.d.)?"

In Proverbs 13:4 (NLT) the Bible says: *"Lazy people want much but get little, but those who work hard will prosper."*

Choose to be the best version of you every day.

June 19th

Wrath

Have you ever felt uncontrolled anger or hatred towards somebody who has wronged you? Many people hold onto anger and it eats them up inside.

The evil one wants us to seek retribution for wrongs committed against us. We are called to release that anger. After all, God forgives us, even when we deserve His wrath.

After being asked how many times one should forgive a brother, Jesus says to Peter in Matthew 18:22 (NASB): *"Jesus said to him, 'I do not say to you, up to seven times, but up to seventy times seven.'"*

Let's pray that there will be more forgiveness and less wrath among us.

June 20th

Envy

Resentful longing for someone else's possession, qualities or luck is the definition of envy, according to dictionary.com. Most people experience this at some point in their lives. Envy can destroy friendships, bank accounts and lives.

This life is not a competition against others or one's self. It is about sharing the Gospel with the non-believing world.

In Galatians 5:26 (NIV) the Bible says: *"Let us not become conceited, provoking and envying each other."*

Be grateful for the Lord's blessings and you won't have time to be jealous of anybody else.

Pride

Pride is a double-edged sword. On one side, we should be proud of a job well done, but on the other side, we should not boast about our accomplishments as if we are better than someone else. We can identify with someone who is prideful and sometimes be the person in the mirror.

Lucifer is a prime example of someone who was so proud of himself, his ways, his honor and own glory that he wanted to be God.

The Bible says in 1 Peter 5:5 (NASB): *"You younger men, likewise, be subject to your elders; and all of you, clothe yourselves with humility toward one another, for God is opposed to the proud but gives grace to the humble."*

Practicing humility is a great way to stay away from selfish pride.

June 22nd

God's Timing

Events occur according to God's plan not ours. If we accept this, we'd have less stress in our lives.

When preparing for The First Annual Walk for Water, which highlights the struggles in African countries to obtain clean water, I worried nobody would participate and the people in Africa won't receive the water they desperately need through Living Water Ohio.

In Acts 1:7 (NLT) Jesus tells the apostles: *"He replied, 'The Father alone has the authority to set those dates and times, and they are not for you to know.'"*

We control where we put our trust for answers, not in the timing of the answers.

June 23rd

Maximum Security

At the Kentucky Derby horse race, bettors put down money in hopes their chosen horse will win. The year Maximum Security apparently crossed the finish line first, a further review found the real winner was Country House. Many people's hopes were dashed over the disqualification, while others' dreams came true with the longshot winning the race.

People try to find security through a variety of different avenues. But there is only one way to find and receive true security: placing your faith in God.

Ephesians 1:13 (ESV) says: *"In Him you also, when you heard the word of truth, the gospel of your salvation, and believed in Him, were sealed with the promised Holy Spirit."*

Know that you have been sealed with God when you receive salvation!

June 24th

Prayer of the Week

Philippians 4:6 (NIV)

"Do not be anxious about anything, but in every situation, by prayer and petition, with thanksgiving, present your requests to God."

This week replace all your anxieties with prayers to God. Ask God to take what burdens you and replace those things with joy and hope.

June 25th

Jesus

How much power is in an "I AM" statement when someone is talking. The person is not suggesting that they may be something or hinting at possibilities. The person is making a bold statement in affirming what they are. Jesus made eight "I AM" statements.

At the time the people refused to accept them as truths and eventually put Him to death for making such blasphemous statements. Today, there are still many who deny that Jesus was the Messiah or the way to eternity with God.

In John 14:6 (New American Standard Bible) Jesus says: *"I am the way, and the truth and the life; no one comes to the Father but through me."*

Think about who you are and what Jesus has done for you and if you know Him to say boldly "I am a Child of God" and then go proclaim it to the lost world by sharing the love of Jesus.

June 26th

New Day

Today is a new day. It has been 365 days since this date, and you have experienced changes in yourself and those around you. Your friends may have moved, some of your family may have gone to be with the Lord. Whatever the changes, they are part of God's plan for your life.

Right now, wherever you are, this day will be over when the clock strikes midnight. Make the most of this day because once it is gone, you will never get it back.

The Bible says in 2 Corinthians 4:16 (NLT): *"That is why we never give up. Though our bodies are dying, our spirits are being renewed every day."*

Enjoy the adventure God places before you today!

June 27th

Priority

Everyone wants to feel important. When you feel insignificant, it can crush your spirit.

Imagine how God feels when we ignore Him, when He speaks to us and we refuse to acknowledge His existence. Maybe we are too busy to spend any significant amount of time with the One who gave us life and breath. God knows and loves you better than any human.

The Bible says in Hebrews 13:5 (NIV): *"Keep your lives free from the love of money and be content with what you have, because God has said, 'Never will I leave you; never will I forsake you.'"*

Have you put your faith in the One who finds you more important than anything else? If you want this level of importance, please pray this prayer right now: Lord, I am a sinner, I accept that Jesus lived, died and has risen for my sins so that I can be with you in eternity. I know in my heart that Jesus Christ is my Savior. I invite the Holy Spirit into my life to guide me on the path you have for me. I thank you and praise you. In Jesus name I pray, Amen!

June 28th

Fully Trust

Most of us want to control everything and rely on ourselves. Some of us have been hurt by someone we trusted or let down by someone they relied on to accomplish something on their behalf. Others want to control everything for the power and prestige that comes with being in charge.

Learning to trust someone can be very difficult to accept. Trusting makes us vulnerable and can be devastating in certain situations.

Proverbs 3:5 (ESV) says *"Trust in the Lord with all your heart, and do not lean on your own understanding."*

June 29th

Preventative Maintenance

To properly maintain a home, vehicle or our bodies, we must take the proper measures to prevent major damage. Issues may still arise during the lifecycle of any of these items, but when maintained at regular intervals, warning signs may arise before requiring a major repair.

If we apply this simple approach in our relationships with others and God, most issues could be resolved quickly and with less damaging results. Neglect leads to deterioration.

The Bible says in 1 John 1:7 (NIV): *"But if we walk in the light, as He is in the light, we have fellowship with one another, and the blood of Jesus, His Son, purifies us from all sin."*

Take time to maintain your relationship with others and God.

June 30th

Love Overcomes

It's easy to lose your temper and turn on someone who is attacking you physically, emotionally or spiritually. Disciplining ourselves in what the Bible teaches about love can assist in defeating the enemies we face in this world.

Approaching an enemy with the word of God and love can diffuse tense situations.

The Bible says in Romans 12:21 (NLT): *"Don't let evil conquer you but conquer evil by doing good."*

My prayer is that you will use the skills God has equipped you with to overcome.

July

July 1st

Prayer of the Week

James 5:16 (NLT)

"Confess your sins to each other and pray for each other so that you may be healed. The earnest prayer of a righteous person has great power and wonderful results."

This week confess your sins daily to a friend and ask them to do likewise. Then pray for them and relieve them of their errors in judgement.

July 2nd

Mid-Year

Today marks the middle of the year. So far, 182 have passed and 182 remain except for leap year. Take stock now of what you have done and what you plan to do for the rest of the year.

God laid it on my heart to write these devotions for GIV365 and to compile them into a book. I broke down this task into a daily activity that helps me as much as the people receiving God's message through them.

The Bible says in Philippians 3:14 (NASB): *"I press on toward the goal for the prize of the upward call of God in Christ Jesus."*

My prayer is that God will be at the center of your hopes and dreams as you reach to meet your personal goals for the year! Have a blessed Mid-Year!

July 3rd

Overwhelm

The definition of 'overwhelm' is to overpower with superior forces and to cover or bury beneath a mass of something, according to Dictionary.com. The situation you face determines which definition speaks to you.

During a battle, one side is overwhelmed by destruction and the victor feels overwhelmed with a great victory. Do you feel overwhelmed right now? If so, are you the victor or the defeated?

The Bible says in Romans 8:37 (NASB): *"But in all things we overwhelmingly conquer through Him who loved us."*

You may face defeat but know that you have victory in Jesus Christ!

July 4th

Independence Day

On July 4, 1776, the thirteen American colonies declared their freedom from the monarch of Britain, giving birth to what is now the United States of America. Today is a celebration of how far our nation has come and, more importantly, understanding that freedom has a price.

The United States was formed as "One Nation Under God" and our currency has "IN GOD WE TRUST" in bold letters. You can declare your freedom in Christ no matter where you live!

The Bible says in 2 Corinthians 3:17 (NIV): *"Now the Lord is the Spirit, and where the Lord is, there is Freedom."*

Know that you have freedom in God and that sometimes that freedom comes with a responsibility to live according to His plan.

July 5th

Too Much, Too Little

Do you tend to find fault in everything or know someone who does? Chances are you do or have been that person at some point. People who complain about the cold during winter are also complain about the heat of summer.

For me, nothing was ever good enough and I always had a higher standard than anyone could meet, myself included. This still creeps into my life but having a close relationship with God allows me to quickly squash those thoughts. I now focus on how blessed I am.

The Bible says in Philippians 2:14 (NLT): *"Do everything without complaining and arguing."*

Replace complaints with counting blessings.

The Bug Bag

How often do you lose your patience?

I was recently shopping for a bag to catch the beetles eating the leaves of the plants in our garden and orchard. To be efficient, I used an app to find the correct store aisle – but the bug bag wasn't there. I requested help several times to no avail, so I purchased the item online. Nobody I encountered in the large store knew where the bags were. After 40 minutes, a young woman finally directed me to the bug bags. My patience wore thin during this time because I believe the employees should know where things are located, but who am I to judge? This interaction provided a lesson about being patient.

The Bible says in Ephesians 4:2 (NASB): *"With all humility and gentleness, with patience, showing tolerance for one another in love,"*

Patience is important and we all need to practice it regularly.

July 7th

Sunburn

When someone plans to spend time in the sun, it is wise to wear protection in the form of clothes, sunscreen, hat and eyewear. Exposure for prolonged periods of time results in a sunburn.

There are all kinds of warning against various behaviors and the results if protection is not used, yet people continue to ignore the warning labels.

The Bible says in Proverbs 2:11 (NIV): *"Discretion will protect you, and understanding will guard you."*

Use the knowledge in the Bible as a guide to guard against unwanted outcomes.

July 8th

Prayer of the Week

1 Timothy 2:1 (NLT)

"I urge you, first of all, to pray for all people. Ask God to help them; intercede on their behalf and give thanks for them."

Pray for all of mankind this week and that the lost will have ears to hear and eyes to see God.

July 9th

Sunset

God is magnificent in all that He does. Just look at the sky, especially near sunset and see the brilliant artistry of His workmanship.

The Bible says in Psalm 19:1 (NLT): *"The heavens proclaim the glory of God. The skies display His craftsmanship."*

Take a moment to watch the sunset this evening and stand in awe of God!

July 10th

Judge and Jury

Who are we to be judge and jury at any time?

Governments around the world have ways of upholding laws and rendering punishments for those found guilty. We think we can look at a situation, know all sides and be objective based when each side of an argument has its own version of the truth. God knows all sides.

The Bible says in Luke 6:37 (NIV): *"Do not judge, and you will not be judged. Do not condemn and you will not be condemned. Forgive, and you will be forgiven."*

Think twice about judging others – one day we will all be judged.

July 11th

Worry About the Future

Do you allow worry to creep into your thoughts? When this happens, a door opens and invites in all kinds of other worries. Worry is not a friend and this door should remain closed and locked with the key thrown away.

I used to worry about everything – it was all-consuming and exhausting. The only result was illness. Making myself sick in fearing the unknown is no way to live. If you can identify, there is hope!

Jesus says in Matthew 6:34 (NASB): *"So do not worry about tomorrow; for tomorrow will care for itself. Each day has enough trouble of its own."*

Focus on overcoming your present trouble, conquer worry and move forward!

July 12th

In God We Trust

On this day in 1955, President Eisenhower signed a bill requiring the use of the inscription "In God We Trust" on all United States paper money (In god we trust, n.d.). The motto of the United States is the phrase too. When you decide to put your trust in God, you get instant access to the Holy Spirit and His kingdom.

There is no waiting process to receive your salvation. God accepts you as soon as you sincerely ask for forgiveness of your sins and accept that Jesus Christ died for you.

The Bible says in 2 Corinthians 1:22 (NIV): *"Set His seal of ownership on us and put His Spirit in our hearts as a deposit, guaranteeing what is to come."*

Trust that you are a child of God and have the Holy Spirit living in you!

July 13th

Headaches

There are several types of headaches caused by illness or stress or unknown reasons. When your head hurts it can be a minor inconvenience or excruciating ordeal.

I get migraines once or twice a year, sometimes with an aura in my vision. I take it to the Lord knowing He will carry me through the unpleasant experience.

The Bible says in Psalm 34:19 (NASB): *"Many are the afflictions of the righteous, but the Lord delivers him out of them all."*

Rest assured that the Lord God Almighty will rescue you from your affliction.

July 14th

Testing the Spirit

Living with the Holy Spirit allows you to discern the true spirit. At times, it's difficult to discern when a small percentage of evil is mixed in with the truth.

Tozer, A. W., & Snyder, J. L. (2014) writes in 'The Crucified Life,' "The most dangerous spiritual guide is the person who is 95% true to the scriptures. Remember it is not the truth that hurts you, rather it is the evil. The 95% truth is trumped by the 5% of evil."

The Bible says in 1 John 4:1 (NLT): *"Dear friends, do not believe everyone who claims to speak by the Spirit. You must test them to see if the spirit they have comes from God. For there are many false prophets in the world."*

The Holy Spirit of God can and will only speak 100% truth.

July 15th

Prayer of the Week

Psalm 86:1 (NLT)

"Bend down, O Lord, and hear my prayer, answer me, for I need your help."

Practice listening to God's answer to your prayers this week. Know His answer will be in your best interest.

July 16th

Excuses

When the Lord calls on you to do something for Him, do you ask to be excused or come up with excuses?

I found myself asking to be excused from a public service commitment due to a client conflict but was denied. At the same time, I texted a friend a few excuses why I couldn't be present at group meeting. When I read what I wrote, I followed with a text saying, "Excuses," and ended up at the meeting.

One day soon, we will all give an account to God for why we need to be excused from going to Hell. Will you make excuses, accept responsibility or ask to be excused?

The Bible says in Genesis 3:12 (ESV): *"The man said, 'The woman whom you gave to be with me, she gave me fruit of the tree, and I ate.'"*

Let's accept personal responsibility for our actions today and stop making excuses.

July 17th

Ripe Fruit

When fruit is immature, it tastes bitter. If the fruit ripens and no one eats, it rots. There is a perfect time to eat fruit.

People who live in harmony with the Holy Spirit are like ripe fruit and most people love the perfect fruit. People who are immature or too overbearing can be like rotten fruit.

The Bible says in Galatians 5:22-23 (NLT): *"But the Holy Spirit produces this kind of fruit in our lives: Love, Joy, Peace, Patience, Kindness, Goodness, Faithfulness, Gentleness, and Self-Control. There is no law against these things!"*

My prayer for you is to grow in all nine characteristics of the Holy Spirit and thus bear the perfect fruit.

July 18th

Deep Roots

Giant sequoias are massive trees that can grow to 300 feet tall with a diameter of nearly 40 feet. These gigantic trees can weigh up to 2.5 million pounds and has a relatively shallow root structure of 10 feet deep. However, this root system sprawls underground throughout an entire acre, intertwining with other sequoias to provide greater strength against storms. The trees can also withstand fire with 3-inch-thick bark.

The Christian life is filled with storms and fires that come to destroy what God is doing in and through you. However, the Bible says in Ecclesiastes 4:12 (ESV): *"And though a man might prevail against one who is alone, two will withstand him – a threefold cord is not quickly broken."*

Become deeply rooted in and with other Christians so that you can withstand the battles that come your way.

July 19th

Busyness

How many activities do you find yourself participating in just to stay busy, not necessarily doing with or for a specific purpose? Plans to do things with friends, football games to watch, television programs to keep up with and we must not forget the news, especially the social media news.

God has great plans for your life and sometimes it may mean removing frivolous activities to accomplish His will. If you feel like you are too busy, but not accomplishing meaningful things it may be time to reassess your what your time is being used to do.

The Bible tells us in Proverbs 19:21 (NIV): *"Many are the plans in a person's heart, but it is the Lords purpose that prevails."*

Take time to assess why you are so busy and ask God to realign your time to fulfill His purposes for your life.

Fatigue

A common symptom as a result of the busyness described in yesterday's devotion is fatigue. One can be so involved in what God is doing that they do not have the luxury of extended periods of rest.

The bible says in Isaiah 40:29 (NLT): *"He gives power to the weak and strength to the powerless."*

Turn to God in times of weakness and find the strength you need to continue to do great things for His kingdom.

July 21st

Trading Truth for Lies

There are many different ideas believed to be true throughout societies around the world that contradict the gospel. People will worship idols and put other things before God. One doesn't have to look to far to see these lies among their circle of friends or colleagues in most instances.

The Bible tells us in Romans 1:25 (NIV): *"They exchanged the truth about God for a lie and worshipped and served created things rather than the Creator-who is forever praised. Amen."*

Refuse the temptation to replace the sovereign God with something less than He.

July 22nd

Prayer of the Week

1 John 5:15 (NLT)

"And since we know He hears us when we make our requests, we also know that He will give us what we ask for."

Pray to God with confidence knowing He is honoring your requests according to His will.

July 23rd

Well-equipped

It is important to have the right equipment when starting a project. If a carpenter doesn't have a tape measure to get the proper lengths for cuts, the project won't fit together as planned.

The same is true for Christians who go out into the world to share the gospel of Jesus Christ. If a person shares their love of God without the Bible or guidance from the Holy Spirit, the results may not be fruitful.

The Bible says in Hebrews 13:21 (NASB): *"Equip you in every good thing to do His will, working in us that which is pleasing in His sight, through Jesus Christ, to whom be the glory forever and ever. Amen."*

Go into the world prepared to do God's will in every situation.

July 24th

Just Breathe

Breathing is essential to human life, but there are moments when people hold their breath.

When someone feels pain, anticipation, fear, and anger, people tend to not breathe. Practice taking a few, slow breaths in and out to calm your mind during high-stress moments.

Doctors tell birthing mothers to breathe. Patients with post-traumatic stress disorder do breathing exercises and my wife tells me to breath when I feel pain because I tend to hold my breath – as if it will make things better.

The Bible says in John 20:22 (ESV): *"And when He said this, He breathed on them and said to them, 'Receive the Holy Spirit.'"*

There's power in breathing. The next time you face stress, pain or anxious thoughts, just breathe.

July 25th

Work Partner

God wants to work with you on everything! God yearns to be your workout friend, study buddy and business partner. Too often, people rely so much on themselves they are distracted from the help that is readily available upon request.

The Bible says in Philippians 2:13 (NASB): *"For it is God who is at work in you, both to will and to work for His good pleasure."*

Invite God to your next workout, study session and business meeting to see what His will is for your life.

July 26th

Truth of Fiction

More than 50 years ago, American astronauts landed on the moon – Neil Armstrong was the first to stepped onto the surface. Although there are many books, movies and articles about this amazing part of history, some believe the moon landing was a Hollywood production that never happened. Others worship the men who accomplished the moon landing.

The Bible is also an account of history.

Jesus says in John 8:32 (NIV): *"Then you will know the truth, and the truth will set you free."*

The Spirit of God will help you uncover the truth.

July 27th

What Lies Ahead

Do you look in the rearview mirror of life constantly? We all need to keep our eyes on the road ahead so we can maneuver through the present.

Like me, you may find yourself looking back at mistakes for the sole purpose of not making them again. My future goals in Christ are more important than my past mistakes and failures. It is much easier to overcome when not dwelling on the past.

The Bible says in Philippians 3:13 (NLT): *"No, dear brothers and sisters, I have not achieved it, but I focus on this one thing: Forgetting the past and looking forward to what lies ahead."*

Plan for future goals with God in mind, instead of dwelling on past failures or successes you have experienced.

July 28th

Sharing the Gospel

Even with current technology, there are people who have not heard about Jesus Christ. Our church recently sent a team to a remote part of Kenya to share the Gospel with an unreached group of people.

The Bible says in John 20:21 (NASB): *"So Jesus said to them, 'Peace be with you; as the Father sent Me, I also send you.'"*

We sent our mission team with prayers for safe travel, strength and wellness, as they helped people know Christ.

Prayer of the Week

Matthew 6:7 (CEV)

"When you pray, don't talk on and on as people do who don't know God. They think God likes to hear long prayers."

Pray specific, short prayers to God this week by eliminating endless repetition...as if He weren't listening or understanding you the first time.

July 30th

Spirit of Love

How often do you express love in the way of Jesus and God? It may be easy to love those close to you, but what about your enemy or a difficult co-worker?

We are commanded to love everyone, all the time. When times are rough, that when people need more love.

Jesus says in John 15:12 (NIV): *"My command is this: Love each other as I have loved you."*

We are loved by God even when we deserve his wrath. Make a point to love someone who desperately needs it.

July 31st

Freedom in Christ

Are you free or are you a slave to sin? You may have a false sense of being free – free to indulge in the sin that you try to justify in your own mind. When sin creeps into your life, you can become chained to it. You are a prisoner to those transgressions until you run back to God.

The wage of sin is death, but Jesus paid the price on your behalf. Jesus commutes your prison sentence and allows you to enjoy life to its fullest.

Jesus says in John 8:36 (NET): *"So if the son sets you free, you will be really free."*

True freedom is found in Jesus Christ and knowing that He served your sentence on your behalf.

August

August 1st

Spirit of Joy

Are filled with joy? If you are not overflowing with joy right now, there is hope.

When struggles come, joy drains as fast as a cup with no bottom. Jesus wants to be the foundation of your cup so you can be filled and even overflowing into other peoples' cups.

Jesus says in John 15:11 (NLT): *"I have told you these things so that you will be filled with My joy. Yes, your joy will overflow!"*

Allow Jesus to fill you with His joy every day.

WWJD

Do angry or peaceful thoughts fill your mind? Chances are if you are angry, your actions will reflect anger. If you are filled with peace, you will have calm actions.

What Would Jesus Do? (WWJD) is a popular saying: before acting, stop and ask, "What would Jesus do?" Answering this question before reacting to a situation allows us to think about the next step.

Colossians 3:15 (NASB) says: *"Let the peace of Christ rule in your hearts, to which indeed you were called in one body; and be thankful."*

Present a peaceful presence to everyone you encounter and notice the results.

August 3rd

Living in the Spirit

Do you consider yourself to be living in the Holy Spirit? If so, how does it show up in your life and the encounters you have with the people around you?

Many of us claim to be guided by the Spirit, yet we sin with no reflection of the Spirit shining through us for the world to see.

The Bible says in Galatians 5:25 (NASB): *"If we live by the Spirit, let us also walk by the Spirit."*

Be filled with the presence and power of the Holy Spirit.

August 4th

Spirit of Patience

Do you consider yourself a patient person in traffic when running late? How about a delayed flight or somebody antagonizing you when you are already impatient? Or even this list of questions delaying your busy day with so little time to read this 2-minute – now 2.5-minute devotional. Did you answer all the questions?

Bearing provocation, annoyance, misfortune, delay, hardship, pain, etc. with fortitude and calm and without complaint, anger or the like (Patient, n.d.)

The Bible says in Galatians 6:9 (NLT): *"So let's not get tired of doing what is good. At just the right time we will reap a harvest of blessing if we don't give up."*

Be patient in everything knowing God has a blessing for you at the right time.

August 5th

Prayer of the Week

Psalm 19:14 (NIV)

"May these words of my mouth and this meditation of my heart be pleasing in your sight, Lord, my Rock and my Redeemer."

Pray in a way that shows a heart filled with love and reverence for your savior this week. Give God the glory He and only He deserves.

August 6th

Spirit of Goodness

What is your definition of goodness and how does it show up in your life daily?

The excellence of quality is one definition of goodness according to Dictionary.com. Now, answer the second part of the question again. Did the list in your daily life change after reading this definition?

We should strive for goodness in all we do. When fatigued, we often settle for mediocrity.

The Bible says in Psalm 23:6 (NASB): *"Surely Your goodness and love will follow me all the days of my life, and I will dwell in the house of the Lord forever."*

Bring goodness to all your relationships just like God does and make note of the changes.

August 7th

Spirit of Faithfulness

The Bible is inspired by God and He is true to His word. Can the same be said about you and your word to others?

Every day in this broken world we see people breaking promises in business, family and friendships. Chances are you've been unfaithful in a promise to someone and the same has been done to you.

The Bible says in 2 Timothy 3:16 (NLT): *"All scripture is inspired by God and is useful to teach us what is true and to make us realize what is wrong in our lives. It corrects us when we are wrong and teaches us to do what is right."*

Learn from the Bible how to do what is right and be strong in your faithfulness in all areas of life.

August 8th

Spirit of Self-Control

Do you prohibit yourself from indulging in activities that go against God? Consuming to much alcohol, using illegal drugs, viewing pornography and thousands of other activities plague the world today.

I used to be reckless and because I lacked control over myself. Drinking alcohol would make matters even worse when I was in my 20s. I am thankful I allowed the Holy Spirit to enter my life to help me overcome my lack of self-restraint.

The Bible says in Proverbs 25:28 (ESV): *"A man without self-control is like a city broken into and left without walls."*

Whatever your area of self-indulgence, the Holy Spirit can help you overcome.

August 9th

Wisdom from God

Throughout history, wise people have sold their knowledge in the form of books, lectures and seminars. Otherwise, people give it away to help others.

Parents sometimes share wisdom with their children only after a child misbehaves and needs to be corrected. The wisdom may fall on deaf ears when a child is upset.

James 1:5 Bible (ESV) says: *"If any of you lacks wisdom, let him ask God, who gives generously to all without reproach, and it will be given him."*

If you need some fresh wisdom, simply ask God.

August 10th

Spirit of Kindness

Do you display kindness to the poor, an elderly person, a neighbor in need of help or hold the door for someone? Showing someone kindness is good for the receiver and the giver.

Being kind used to be a big struggle for me. I knew what it meant and how to do it, but anger and frustration about my personal situations in life made it difficult to show other people favor. Thankfully, I moved past this low point in my life and I am able, willing and do behave in a friendly manner toward others.

The Bible says in Proverbs 19:17 (NIV): *"Whoever is kind to the poor lends to the Lord, and He will reward them for what they have done."*

Exercising kindness to all you encounter today, not because of the reward, but because you will become fit. Have a blessed day.

August 11th

Triumph over Tragedy

My brother-in-law had turned 47 a week before running a 5k with his wife and two of his children in Wapakoneta, OH to celebrate the 50th anniversary of the first man on the moon. No one knew this father, brother, uncle, husband and friend to many would take one last step on Earth and one giant leap into the arms of Jesus.

When this occurred, I was in the final stages of a mission trip to Kenya to plant a church and share the gospel of Jesus Christ with unreached people. There were so many reasons I could think of not to go. God orchestrated all the details prior to this tragedy. The triumph came when I connected with a man who thought he could continue to put off accepting Christ until he heard about my brother-in-law's story. None of us are guaranteed another day or even another breath. With my wife's blessing – and the blessing of God – I travelled to Kenya.

The Bible says in Romans 8:28 (NIV): *"And we know that in all things God works for the good of those who love Him, who have been called according to His purpose."*

God has a plan to bring triumph out of your tragedy.

August 12th

Prayer of the Week

1 Timothy 2:2 (NLT)

"Pray this way for kings and all who are in authority so that we can live peaceful and quiet lives marked by godliness and dignity."

This week pray for the leaders of all the governments throughout the world and that they may come to know Christ and lead their nations with love in their hearts.

August 13th

Work of Art

Humans are the same inside and out. Beyond common traits, we are created with specific details that separate us from one another. Skin color, blood types and fingerprints are a few physical traits that define each person.

God designed you and placed you where you are for an important role in life. Are you fulfilling that role and accepting the challenge to do His will in your life? You were not created on an assembly line for an ordinary purpose.

The Bible says in Ephesians 2:10 (NLT): *"For we are God's masterpiece. He has created us anew in Christ Jesus, so we can do the good things He planned for us long ago."*

You are a priceless work of art created to do great things on Earth!

August 14th

Imperfect

It might be hard to grasp the idea that all of us are imperfect. Societies, companies and even churches set standards for perfection. If the minimum standard is not met, the person, product or member may be cast aside.

The ultimate standard of perfection is Jesus Christ. By this standard, we should all be deemed unworthy. God wants us to show one another the same compassion and forgiveness He has shown us despite all our flaws.

The Bible says in Ephesians 4:32 (NASB): *"Be kind to one another, tender-hearted, forgiving each other, just as God in Christ also has forgiven you."*

Connect with someone who needs to be forgiven because love is perfected in forgiveness.

Numb

Have you ever had an appendage fall asleep or
received numbing medication before some treatment?
The lack of feeling lasts for a short time and then, as the
medication wears off, there is pain or tingling.

The world we live in today seems like everyone has
been numbed against love and the only feeling left is
hate. Imagine a world opposite of this example. Hate
would not even be in the vocabulary.

The Bible says in Revelation 21:4 (NIV): *"He will wipe
every tear from their eyes. There will be no more death or
mourning or crying or pain, for the older order of things has
passed away."*

Until that day comes, medicate and help eradicate hate.

August 16th

Super-Superabundantly

A team of nine from the United States embarked on a mission to Kenya with high hopes that God would do great things in and through us. Our God never fails us. With many people praying and local Kenyans accompanying us, God showed up in all His majesty.

In the short time the team was in Kenya, 232 people accepted Jesus into their lives. Plus 330 people received medical care from the medical staff, 60 individuals were baptized, and 38 people committed to being members of the new church planted in the remote area.

The Bible says in Ephesians 3:20 (NLT): *"Now all glory to God, who is able, through His mighty power at work within us, to accomplish infinitely more than we might ask or think."*

Trust and know that God will do a mighty work in and through you more powerful than you can imagine.

August 17th

Strength in Numbers

Christians are under attack from the evil. The devil uses anything he can to get to us. When we travel together in a group or as a team of Christians, we are a great army able to defeat the attacks.

After arriving back in the United States from a Kenya mission trip, the group dispersed to be with their families. Satan immediately tried to take advantage of the individuals in a variety of ways. The strategy of the evil one is to divide and conquer.

The Bible says in 1 Corinthians 12:12 (NIV): *"Just as a body, though one, has many parts, but all its many parts form one body, so it is with Christ."*

Find strength in a group or team and always have the strength to defeat the evil one.

Blueprints

How often do you consult God on the work you intend to do? Many people start work and then consult God when problems arrive with their initial plan.

Before a construction project begins, a blueprint needs to be approved – the building doesn't come first. The same goes for our plans. We should go to God with a plan and get approval or guidance prior to embarking on the project.

The Bible says in Proverbs 16:3 (NIV): *"Commit to the Lord whatever you do, and He will establish your plans."*

Submit your blueprints to God before you start the work.

Prayer of the Week

1 John 1:9 (NIV)

"If we confess our sins, He is faithful and just and will forgive us our sins and purify us from all unrighteousness."

When praying this week, be sure to include step one in the process. Honestly call out the sin in your life and know that God will make you as clean.

August 20th

Askew

The leaning tower of Pisa was built in Italy with an unstable foundation and, as a result, the structure leans nearly four degrees. Have you ever felt like you were not on a stable foundation?

God prompted me to start my day by reading the Bible and praying. When I miss my Bible time, I later realize something about my day is off. That foundation first thing every day ensures I am not leaning away from my Father.

Jesus says in Matthew 7:24 (NIV): *"Therefore everyone who hears these words of mine and puts them into practice is like a wise man who built his house on the rock."*

God's foundation will help you stand upright and guide you through your day.

August 21st

Events

Every moment of every day since the beginning of time, some events bring great joy while others bring tremendous sadness.

Whether you are celebrating a victory or trying to survive after a defeat, your strength is coming from the same source.

The Bible says in Psalm 18:1 (NASB): *"I love you, O Lord, my strength."*

Love the One who provides you with the strength you need for all the events of your life.

August 22nd

Be Brave

Are you facing a situation you fear? It could be mistreatment at work, anxiety about an upcoming quiz or news of a diagnosed illness.

When faced with reality, we can choose the path of the weakness or the path of the strength. The weak path is filled with ways to discourage you and give you doubts about your ability to overcome. The path of strength is accompanied by thoughts and encouragement in abundance to carry you through to the end.

The Bible says in Deuteronomy 31:6 (NIV): *"Be strong and courageous. Do not be afraid or terrified because of them, for the Lord your God goes with you; He will never leave you nor forsake you."*

Find courage in every situation you face.

August 23rd

The Rooster Crow

How often do you deny Jesus by your lifestyle and bad habits? Paul, a faithful servant of Jesus, denied Him three times in one evening after Paul assured Jesus he would never fall away.

Jesus knows your heart and your habits that prevent you from being close to Him, just like He knew Paul would deny Him.

The Bible says in Matthew 26:34 (NASB): *"Jesus said to him, 'Truly I say to you that this very night before a rooster crows, you will deny me three times.'"*

Acknowledge Jesus in all you say and do.

August 24th

God's Will, Not Yours

Praying with a heart aligned to God's will for you can be a daunting task. We want and desire things to make us feel better or more comfortable but are outside the will of God.

I used to pray for things I thought would be best for me, but now I know God has much greater things in store for me than I could ever imagine. Seeking His will above my own shifted many aspects of who I once was.

The Bible says in James 4:3 (NLT): *"And even when you ask, you don't get it because your motives are all wrong – you want only what will give you pleasure."*

Start praying for God's will in your life and be amazed at the answers you will receive.

August 25th

Gospel of Peace

The foundation on which you stand needs protection. Without the gospel of Jesus Christ, we would not have feet to stand up to evil.

If you go into battle with hatred in your heart, you are selfishly fighting the battle on your own and not allowing peace to flow in and through you from the Holy Spirit.

The Bible says in Ephesians 6:15 (NIV): *"...and now your feet fitted with the readiness that that comes from the Gospel of peace."*

Allow the Spirit of God to fill you from head to toe with the strength and peace that comes from the word of God.

August 26th

Prayer of the Week

1 Chronicles 16:11 (NASB)

"Seek the Lord and His strength; seek His face continually."

Pray for closeness to your heavenly Father and for His will in your life.

August 27th

Helmet of Salvation

Your head is where you process thoughts and where your mind resides. This vital area needs around the clock protection from evil and sinful thoughts trying to enter your mind and heart.

One of the most powerful tools Satan uses against you is distorting perceptions of truth and reality. The mind is a powerful tool and can be used for good or evil.

The Bible says in Ephesians 6:17 (NIV): *"Take the helmet of salvation and the sword of the Spirit, which is the word of God."*

Be careful what you allow to enter your thoughts and heart.

August 28th

Pray Always

How often do you put on the full armor of God thinking you're covered? With the full armor of God, you're prepared for evil and in close fellowship with the Holy Spirit.

The Bible says in Ephesians 6:18 (NLT): *"Pray in the Spirit at all times and on every occasion. Stay alert and be persistent in your prayers for all believers everywhere."*

Yield to the power of the Holy Spirit in you to help you overcome your enemy!

August 29th

90-Day Challenge

Although Thanksgiving is three months away, it will be here before you know it. I challenge you to journal each day a reason you are thankful and give praise to God. While journaling, watch for a difference in your outlook and attitude.

The Bible says in Psalms 95:2 (NET): *"Let's enter His presence with thanksgiving! Let's shout out to Him in celebration!"*

Start giving thanks today to God for all the wonderful things He has given you!

Sin, Repent, Repeat

Do you get tired of doing laundry? The spiritual washing machine works the same way: you sin, repent and repeat it all over again. Like clothing, we start to wear down and fall apart from the repetitive sin in our lives.

As a child, I would purposefully play in the mud to see how dirty I could get, much to the displeasure of my mother. As I grew older, it was the same with my sins and God. My own gratification was more important than how it made God feel.

The Bible says in 2 Corinthians 7:1 (NIV): *"Therefore, since we have these promises, dear friends, let us purify ourselves from everything that contaminates body and spirit, perfecting holiness out of reverence from God."*

Refrain from sin, avoiding guilt, please your Father in heaven.

August 31st

Shield of Faith

Pick up your shield and protect against the aerial assault from the master of deception. Faith is having confidence and trust in someone or something. We must trust that God is helping us behind the scenes and acts as our shield against such attacks.

I pray for a wall of protection for my family and friends against the schemes of evil people. Relying on God by faith is difficult for the non-believing world – and sometimes the believers, too.

The Bible says in Ephesians 6:16 (NASB): *"In addition to all, taking up the shield of faith with which you will be able to extinguish all the flaming arrows of the evil one."*

May your faith in the Lord Jesus Christ be your shield during the attacks from evil.

September

September 1st

Washing of Feet

Wearing sandals is common in warm weather regions, which leads to dirty feet. In Jesus' time, servants washed the feet of guests.

Can you imagine washing the feet of everyone who visited your home? The thought may make you cringe, yet many people, including Jesus, did this act of service.

The Bible says in John 13:5 (NASB): *"Then He poured water into the basin and began to wash the disciples' feet and to wipe them with the towel with which He was girded."*

What tasks are you resisting even though God wants you to do them?

September 2nd

Prayer of the Week

Matthew 26:41 (NIV)

"Watch and pray so that you will not fall into temptation. The spirit is willing, but the flesh is weak."

Find a place this week that's not too comfortable so as you pray, you do not drift off to sleep.

September 3rd

You Are Not Your Own

Ownership (n.d.) gives someone the legal right of possession. People take ownership of cars, houses, businesses etc. Truly we are only entrusted by God to oversee what He gives us while we are here on Earth.

The world says your body is yours – do what you feel. Both believers and non-believers buy into this lie. Prior to allowing the Holy Spirit of God to take up permanent residence in my heart and mind, I put things in and on my body that was contributing to its decay.

The Bible says in 1 Corinthians 6:19 (ESV): *"Or do not know that your body is a temple of the Holy Spirit within you, whom you have from God? You are not your own."*

Take great care of yourself and whatever else God entrusts you to oversee.

Weather the Storm

Hurricane Dorian made history with its impact on the United States. Residents with homes in the path of such powerful storms build houses to withstand the winds and waves that may impact their homes. Although these homes are prepared for major disturbances, that doesn't mean damage won't occur.

Weathering the storm – whether a hurricane or in your own personal life struggles – can help minimize damage. Sin can cause catastrophic damage to anyone in or near the path. There is a way to overcome: by building a strong foundation in Jesus Christ.

Jesus says in Matthew 8:25 (NLT): *"Though the rain comes in torrents and the floodwaters rise and the winds beat against the house, it won't collapse because it is built on bedrock."*

Allow Jesus to be your foundation for weathering the storms you face.

September 5th

Speak Love

Love is a universal language spoken by everyone. Even people who hate someone or something are said to love hating. Love in its purest form is the kind of love God has for everyone.

While on a mission trip to Africa, I needed a translator to communicate my words about Jesus Christ to the village residents. One thing understood without words was my love for the people I encountered. Through my expressions and actions, the Kenyans knew I came in peace and with love in my heart.

Jesus says in John 13:34 (NIV): *"A new command I give you: Love one another. As I have loved you, so you must love one another."*

Practice communicating love to everyone you encounter today through expressions, actions and words.

Run the Course

Ultimate Ninja Warrior is a television show where athletes train relentlessly to better themselves to compete for the championship. These elite athletes run courses filled with obstacles to test strength, endurance, speed, agility and mentality. Some courses are timed, while others must simply be successfully completed. The further an athlete goes into the competition, the more challenging the obstacles become.

Life is like these obstacle courses. You train your body to withstand the tests before you on the course of life. The difference in life is you get more than one chance to complete different segments of the competition. No one knows when the competition will end.

The Bible says in 1 Corinthians 9:26 (NLT): *"So I run with purpose in every step. I am not just shadowboxing."*

Run the course with a goal to meet Jesus at the finish line.

September 7th

Escape Room

Have you participated in an escape room? A room is filled with clues that an individual or group tries to solve like a puzzle. The goal is to escape a before time runs out. The experience can be fun and intense as times runs short.

Temptations are much like an escape room, but sometimes the thrill of the temptation overpowers the desire to escape. People pay the price of the sin because of the thrill it brings them.

The Bible says in 1 Corinthians 10:13 (NLT): *"The temptations in your life are no different from what others experience. And God is faithful. He will not allow the temptation to be more than you can stand. When you are tempted, he will show you a way out so that you can endure."*

Know that your God provides all the clues deliver you from enticements.

September 8th

Promises

Have you had a promise to you broken or broken a promise made to someone? Children promise to behave and as soon as you turn your back they are misbehaving. A boss makes promises never intending to keep them. A friend promises to meet you and never shows up.

Looking back, I have broken many promises, some with detrimental effects. Promises made to me have been broken. People make promises without thinking of the damage that done when they are broken.

The Bible says in Joshua 21:45 (CEV): *"The Lord promised to do many good things for Israel, and He kept His promise every time."*

Rest assured God's promises to you are always kept.

Prayer of the Week

Proverbs 15:8 (THE MESSAGE)

"God can't stand pious poses, but he delights in genuine prayers."

This week when you pray, don't merely go through the motions. God wants your prayers to be heartfelt and pure.

September 10th

Against the Wind

When sailing a boat, having the wind at your back makes for smooth sailing. On the contrary, sailing directly into the wind is futile. Flying a plane is the opposite. Planes take off against the wind, gaining altitude faster when flying into the wind.

Life is smooth sailing with the wind at your back, but other times it feels like taking off into the wind. The comfortable sailboat stays at the same level, while the plane takes you to a higher place.

The Bible says in Isaiah 48:17 (NIV): *"This is what the Lord says – your Redeemer, the Holy One of Israel: 'I am the Lord your God, who teaches you what is best for you, who directs you in the way you should go.'"*

God wants to take you higher elevations when you think the wind is holding you back.

September 11th

9-1-1

On this date in 2001, the USA was attacked by people filled with hate. In all, 2,997 people were killed and another 6,000 injured. Families were destroyed in an instant because of the evil in others' hearts.

This attack bred hate for the people and nations that helped orchestrate the violence. Like me, you felt angry about what happened to the innocent men, women and children who were going about their daily lives. By feeling that way, the enemy was winning the battle for our hearts and minds.

Jesus says in Luke 6:27-28 (NLT): *"But to you who are willing to listen, I say, love your enemies! Do good to those who hate you. Bless those who curse you. Pray for those who hurt you."*

Today when praying for the families of the victims of 911, also pray for the hearts of our enemies to be changed.

Holiness

You have probably heard the saying, "One rotten apple spoils the bunch." The same is true for us. The apple is like a sick person who is contagious and spreads disease. Sin acts in the same way and spreads quickly throughout a group of believers.

In contrast, one person's holiness does not heal someone else's unholiness. A person is responsible for their own spiritual health. Looking back, I can see the bad influences in my life and how they contributed to my spiritual decline. Those influencers are still in the same place or getting worse, while I am getting better.

The Bible says in Haggai 2:12-13 (NASB): *"'If a man carries holy meat in the fold of his garment, and touches bread with this fold, of cooked food, wine, oil, or any other food, will it become holy?' And the priests answered, 'No.' Then Haggai said, 'If one who is unclean from a corpse touches any of these, will the latter become unclean?' And the priests answered, 'It will become unclean.'"*

Pray for the Holy Spirit to protect you from being infected with contagious sin.

September 13th

Friday the 13th

A quick internet search for the title of this devotional yields a mass of reasons why Friday and 13 are considered unlucky.

My wife and I went on our first date on Friday the 13th and were married on Friday the 13th. Every Friday the 13th, we have a special date to celebrate.

The Bible says in 1 Timothy 1:4 (NLT): *"Don't let them waste their time in endless discussion of myths and spiritual pedigrees. These things only lead to meaningless speculations, which don't help people live a life of faith in God."*

Base your knowledge on the Bible instead of the myths and legends of this world.

September 14th

Temporary Setbacks

Illness, job loss, a broken bone or any number of obstacles you face can seem devastating at the time. Some of the hardships you face last longer than others.

During times of crisis, it's difficult to not focus on the here and now. The dark tunnel seems never-ending, especially if you can't see any light.

The Bible says in 2 Corinthians 4:18 (NIV): *"So we fix our eyes not on what is seen, but on what is unseen since what is seen is temporary, but what is unseen is eternal."*

Keep hope alive during times of difficulty.

September 15th

Oblivious

So many distractions cause us to be unaware of what's going on in the moment. Chances are you will be oblivious to your surroundings at some point today – maybe while you are reading this devotional.

Recently, I was at a stop sign behind a law enforcement officer as an oblivious driver passing without signaling on a double yellow while speeding. The officer acted immediately and pulled over the driver.

Jesus says in Matthew 24:39 (NET): *"And they knew nothing until the flood came and took them away. It will be the same at the coming of the Son of Man."*

It costs nothing to pay attention to God and His teaching, but it can cost you eternity without Him.

September 16th

Prayer of the Week

Matthew 6:9-13 (NIV)

"This, then, is how you should pray: 'Our Father in heaven, hallowed be Your name, your kingdom come, your will be done, on earth as it is in heaven. Give us today our daily bread. And forgive us our debts, as we also forgive our debtors. And lead us not into temptation but deliver us from the evil one.'"

Begin your prayers this week with the example Jesus gave us to follow with the Lord's prayer.

September 17th

Percentages

How much time do you spend reading the Bible in a year? An hour a day equates to just over 15 days or roughly 4% of the year. Add an additional hour per week for going to church and you are just over 17 days or 4.8%. Add another hour for a small group study and you reach 19.5 days or 5.3% of your time learning about God.

Conversely, an average person spends over 25 days or 7% of the year interacting with social media. Social media can be a great place to share with others, but it can also create arguments out of nothing.

The Bible says in Proverbs 18:2 (CEV): *"Fools have no desire to learn, instead, they would rather give their own opinion."*

Spending more time with God can teach you much wisdom.

September 18th

Emergency

Lights and sirens accompany emergency vehicles in times of great distress when swift action is required to prevent further harm.

A friend once told me her family prays whenever they hear sirens. Now, my family also prays for the first responders and others involved in an emergency.

The Bible says in Psalm 71:12 (NLT): *"O God, don't stay away. My God, please hurry to help me."*

Next time you hear sirens, start praying to God on behalf of the victims and the responders.

September 19th

Memorization

"We hold these Truths to be self-evident: that all men are created equal; that they are endowed by their Creator with certain unalienable rights; that among these are life, liberty and the pursuit of happiness." – The Declaration of Independence.

Eighth graders are often required to memorize and recite the preamble to the Declaration of Independence. At the time it seemed like a daunting task, but I still have it memorized after nearly 30 years.

The Bible says in Psalm 119:16 (NIV): *I will delight in your decrees; I will not neglect your word.*

It delights the Lord when you have His word stored in your heart!

September 20th

T.G.I.F.

Thankful God Is Forgiving. If God did not forgive, there would be no hope for human race.

The Bible says in Romans 3:23 (NLT): *"For everyone sinned; we all fall short of God's glorious standard."*

Pray this prayer: Dear God, I thank you for accepting me for who I am and forgiving me of all my sins. Amen!

September 21st

Artificial Intelligence

Technology today understands, analyzes and creates responses by listening to us speaking into electronic devices in our homes and cars. This artificial intelligence even predicts words when we use messaging on mobile devices, putting thoughts into words.

There is an intelligence that exceeds that of humans or computers – our God, who is omniscient and omnipresent and omnipotent. He knows each of us and our hearts.

The Bible says in Psalm 139:4 (NLT): *"You know what I am going to say even before I say it, Lord."*

There is nothing artificial about our wonderful and amazing God.

September 22nd

Necessary Endings

Today marks the ending of summer in the northern hemisphere and the end of winter in the southern hemisphere. Like the seasons across the globe, individuals go through seasons of life.

Babies grow into toddlers and grow out of diapers. Teenagers need a ride everywhere until they earn a driver's license. Young adults finish their formal education to begin a career. The most feared ending is the one nobody wants to talk about…at the end of our lives, we will be at the feet of Jesus giving an account of our life from beginning to end.

The Bible says in Ecclesiastes 7:8 (NET): *"The end of a matter is better than its beginning; likewise, patience is better than pride."*

Look at your life and recognize that endings are necessary for growth and prepare you for the next season.

September 23rd

Prayer of the Week

Psalm 4:1 (NASB)

"Answer me when I call, O God of my righteousness. You have relieved me in my distress; Be gracious to me and hear my prayer."

Pray looking up to the heavens with arms wide open this week as you call out you God. Give your burdens to the only One who can bear all of them.

September 24th

Fulfilling Your Needs

God wants to fulfill your needs. What you think you need and what God knows you need can be completely different.

You may have a communication issue with a co-worker or spouse, and you pray God works on their heart and mind to fall in line with your desired outcome. You may think you need a promotion at work, but God knows you need to learn more in your current position so that you can better equipped when the promotion is finally yours.

The Bible says in Philippians 4:19 (NLT): *"And this same God who takes care of me will supply all your needs from His glorious riches, which have been given to us in Christ Jesus."* God is providing for all your needs, including the ones you don't know about.

Love & Respect

Dr. Emerson Eggerichs, PhD, and his wife Sarah present Love and Respect workshops around the USA. According to Emerson, the woman desires to feel loved and the man wants to be respected. If a woman doesn't feel loved, she won't respect the man; if a man doesn't feel respected, he won't love the woman. This pattern continues until one person decides to break the pattern.

Does this sound like any of your relationships? My wife and I attended this conference early on in our marriage and use the tools we learned to thwart attacks on the special bond we have.

The Bible says in Ephesians 5:33 (CEV): *"So each husband should love his wife as much as he loves himself, and each wife should respect her husband."*

Form a healthy habit of loving and respecting everyone, even those who you think don't deserve it.

September 26th

Pruning

Pruning is defined as removing anything considered superfluous or undesirable, according to Dictionary.com. Consider this definition, then make a list of items to remove from your life.

Jesus says in John 15:2 (NET): *"He takes away every branch that does not bear fruit in me. He prunes every branch that bears fruit so that it will bear more fruit."*

Use the list you created to eliminate needless things so you can grow.

September 27th

Spider Web

Spider webs are nearly invisible unless you have the perfect vantage point -that's now bugs get trapped. Some of us get caught in an invisible trap, and it's difficult to get out.

Temptation is like the invisible web. Everything is fine and, the next thing you know, you're trapped in the evil one's web.

Jesus says in Matthew 6:13 (ESV): *"And lead us not into temptation but deliver us from evil."*

Viewing temptation from the proper angle can help you see and avoid the tangled web of sin.

September 28th

Harvesting

What seeds are planted in your fields? Are they seeds of wrath, hate, anger, greed or lust? Or are you planting seeds of hope, love, grace, joy and self-control?

The saying that you reap what you sow is true. The harvest you receive is a direct result of the seeds you plant. A seed of hate does not produce love.

The Bible says in Galatians 6:7 (NASB): *"Do not be deceived, God is not mocked; for whatever a man sows, this he will also reap."*

Sow good seeds so your harvest will be plentiful.

September 29th

Positive Influence

Social media is a huge influence on our world with gamers, coaches, internet celebrities and other self-proclaimed influencers of anything you can imagine. Some have a positive impact on their followers, who tune in or otherwise buy what they are selling.

The Bible says in 1 Corinthians 10:23 (NLT): *"You say, 'I am allowed to do anything' – but not everything is good for you. You say, 'I am allowed to do anything' – but not everything is beneficial."*

Be sure whatever influences you bring positive and uplifting results.

September 30th

Prayer of the Week

Matthew 7:11 (NLT)

"So, if you sinful people know how to give good gifts to your children, how much more will your heavenly Father give good gifts to those who ask Him."

Pray to the righteous God who knows what we need and is willing to bestow upon us the greatest gifts. After all, He did give us the greatest gift of all, His son.

October

October 1st

Protecting Yourself

There is a war raging all around you. Although you may be feeling peaceful, it is only a matter of time until you are called into the battle.

Military, police, security and emergency medical teams throughout the world are always training for the time they will be called upon to protect and support the people who entrusted them for the mission.

Christians should be studying and training by reading the Word and practicing love always. The mission is the same, although the battles take on many different forms.

The Bible says in Ephesians 6:13 (CEV): *"So put on the armor that God gives. Then when that evil day comes, you will be able to defend yourself. And when the battle is over, you will still be standing firm."*

Prepare yourself for the day that you are called to the battle.

October 2nd

A Great Start

Think about how you start your day and your morning routine. Is it a scattered mess of getting kids ready for school, answering a few emails and scrolling any kind of news feed to see what happened while you rested?

Some suggest people fill themselves with a healthy breakfast before starting the day. While that is a good start, a great start would be getting alone with God to talk and pray.

The start of the day sets the tone for the events that will transpire throughout. My process is to be alone with God for at least the first hour of the day by reading the Bible, two devotionals and praying. It makes a world of difference in how each day goes!

The Bible says in Mark 1:35 (NIV): *"Very early in the morning, while it was still dark, Jesus got up left the house and went off to a solitary place, where He prayed."*

Take a lesson from Jesus, who knows how to start the day in the best way!

October 3rd

Sink or Float

The object of a sinker is to drag something deeper into the darkness of a body of water. A float is designed to keep the object on the float above the surface of the water.

Worry is much like the sinker, dragging a person into a deep abyss. The float is like words of encouragement from fellow believers, helping someone rise.

The Bible says in Proverbs 12:25 (THE MESSAGE): *"Worry weighs us down; a cheerful word picks us up."*

Help save somebody from sinking by giving them something to float on.

October 4th

Victory is Yours

Right now, you face obstacles and doubt you can overcome. Look beyond the obstacle and see the solution.

You, as a Christian, can overcome even the most daunting tasks and roadblocks because you possess the power of the Holy Spirit and the instruction manual.

The Bible says in 1 John 5:4 (NLT): *"For every child of God defeats this evil world, and we achieve this victory through our faith."*

Be strong in your faith, knowing always you are a victorious child of God.

Simply Stated

People spend time, money and energy on self-help books, coaches, mentors and other forms of guidance to fulfill their dreams, desires and wants. These methods can help change your attitude towards life and meeting goals, but there is a simpler approach.

If you take one specific piece of advice the Bible offers, the time and energy wasted trying to get the things you need could be better spent doing more meaningful things.

Luke 12:31 (NLT) says: *"Seek the Kingdom of God above all else, and He will give you everything you need."*

Simplify your life by getting to know God.

The Cowardly Lion

In the movie, The Wizard of Oz, the Cowardly Lion is afraid of everything. In one scene, the lion scares himself with his own tail although real lions rule the jungle and are nicknamed "King of the Beasts."

Looking back at your life, can you find a time when you felt like the lion from the movie? In my life, there are more times than I care to count when I was afraid or feared a situation.

The Bible says in 2 Timothy 1:7 (NASB): *"For God has not given us a spirit of timidity, but of power and love and discipline."*

Take heart knowing God has given you a spirit to take on any situation you face.

October 7th

Prayer of the Week

Psalm 18:6 (NIV)

"In my distress I called to the Lord; I cried to my God for help. From his temple He heard my voice; my cry came before Him, into his ears."

Praying isn't always head bowed and soft whispers in your head. Try opening your eyes to see God all around you and loudly proclaim your need for assistance this week during prayer.

October 8th

I Am

Who are you and what do you stand for? How you describe yourself is more than just a label…parent, Christian, entrepreneur, athlete, spouse, sinner, adult and so many other things.

By affirming who you are, you take ownership of the responsibility for that role. We must also follow it up with action. It is one thing to say you are a Christian, but you must live it out in your daily life.

Jesus says in John 6:35 (ESV): *"Jesus said to them, 'I am the bread of life; whoever comes to Me shall not hunger, and whoever believes in Me shall never thirst.'"*

By affirming your faith in Jesus Christ, you are accepting a great responsibility.

October 9th

Hiding or Seeking

Children from around the world play some version of Hide-and-Seek. One variation is the "It" or seeker counting to 100 while the other players hide. The first one found by the seeker is now "It." My favorite version was adding a home base that all the hiders had to sneak back to without being tagged.

As children grow up and innocence is lost, this game still plays out in daily life. God is always "It" in this version. Some constantly hide thinking they will never be found. Others will constantly seek God and wanting to be "It" with Him. Either way, God knows where you are whether you are hiding or seeking.

The Bible says in Psalm 105:4 (ESV): *"Seek the Lord and His strength; seek His presence continually!"*

Stop hiding from God and seek His companionship perpetually

Frustration

Think about the last time you were frustrated. What was at the core of your dissatisfaction of the circumstance or person that made you feel that way? Was it a driver on your commute or a spouse who couldn't read your mind?

The reasons people become frustrated have more to do with the person who is frustrated than the person or circumstance perceived as the center of the complaint. If a spouse doesn't do something you would like and you haven't even asked them, how are they to know your thoughts?

The Bible says in Colossians 3:13 (NIV): *"Bear with each other and forgive one another if any of you has a grievance against someone. Forgive as the Lord forgave you."*

Sometimes we need to forgive ourselves when we become frustrated.

October 11th

Choosing Teams

During physical education classes, the teacher picks two people to select teams. The athletes in the bunch are usually picked first, followed by friends of the captain and finally those least qualified to win.

Jesus didn't pick his disciples because of their stature, popularity or how qualified they were. He chose the ones with whom He could do great works in and through on His team.

John 15:16 (NLT) says: *"You didn't choose me. I chose you. I appointed you to go and produce lasting fruit, so that the Father will give you whatever you ask for, using my name."*

God has chosen you to be on His team, will you accept His invitation?

October 12th

A Changed Heart

Is there a person in your life that you would deem to be unable to change? Maybe that person is so hooked on drugs or chasing money and the opposite sex that there is no hope that God will ever come into their lives. God can change the hearts of men and women whom you would least expect.

At the end of Acts chapter seven, verses 54-60 Stephen is stoned to death after his sermon to the people. Yet he still asked God to forgive his persecutors. Chapter eight of acts opens with Saul and his approval of the killing of Stephen. Fast forward to Acts nine and Ananias is doubting that Saul can change.

God spoke to Ananias in Acts 9:15 (NIV): *"But the Lord said to Ananias, 'Go! This man is my chosen instrument to proclaim My name to the Gentiles and their kings and to the people of Israel. I will show him how much he must suffer for my name."*

God has the power and ability to change even the most hardened hearts. It is the Christian's responsibility to love and pray for those that need the change of heart.

Grace

The best gift anyone can receive is the gift of grace. Grace (n.d.) is the freely given, unmerited favor and love of God.

You can give grace to those who wrong you – choosing to forgive an undeserving person is what grace is all about.

The Bible says in Ephesians 2:5 (NIV): *"Make us alive with Christ even when we were dead in transgressions – it is by grace you have been saved."*

Give grace to someone who doesn't deserve it every day – starting now!

October 14th

Prayer of the Week

Proverbs 15:29 (CEV)

"The Lord never even hears the prayers of the wicked, but He answers the prayers of all who obey Him."

Obey God with every ounce of your mind, body and soul while praying this week and know that your prayers will be answered.

Heavy Loads

When you go to the grocery store for a few groceries, it's easy to carry them. Chances are you will not attempt to carry a week's worth of groceries without the assistance of a cart.

Why do we sometimes insist on doing things the hard way when it comes to our relationship with Christ? The scribe's teachings were heavy burdens to anyone who wanted to follow. Jesus taught that His ways were much easier to bear than those of the scribes.

Jesus says in Matthew 11:30 (NIV): *"For My yoke is easy and My burden is light."*

Lessen your load by following Jesus' way!

October 16th

No Strings Attached

When a person signs a contract with a cellular phone company, there are usually strings attached to the deal – like the lure of the newest phone for a long-term contract. Breaking the contract results in an exorbitant fee.

Society is plagued with similar tactics among businesses selling goods and services to get an edge on the competition. Men and women try to lure the opposite sex with no-commitment encounters that can come with potentially devastating consequences.

The Bible says in Act 15:11 (NLT): *"We believe that we are all saved the same way, by the undeserved grace of the Lord Jesus."*

Everyone has the same opportunity to accept the gift of salvation through Jesus Christ with no contract or strings attached.

Reboot

Most electronic devices need to be reset at some point due to an error or other malfunction. Think about all the products you use that need to be reset – cars, phones, modems, etc.

People also need a reboot occasionally, most notably their hearts and minds. Work, school, athletics, vacations and even health issues require a reset. When was the last time you shut down your system other than sleep?

The Bible says in Mark 6:31 (NLT): *"Then Jesus said, 'Let's go off by ourselves to a quiet place and rest a while.' He said this because there were so many people coming and going that Jesus and his apostles didn't even have time to eat."*

Be sure to set aside time regularly unwind and decompress your mind, body and soul.

October 18th

Detours

Drivers encounter detours due to road construction or accidents, making for an indirect route to the destination. Some alternate routes may be short while others disrupt the planned journey.

Moses and the people could have reached their destination in a few weeks, if they had taken the most direct route. God had other plans for His people and specific reasons to send them the way He did.

The Bible says in Exodus 13:17 (NIV): *"When Pharaoh let the people go, God did not lead them on the road through the Philistine country, though that was shorter. For God said, 'If they face war, they might change their minds and return to Egypt.'"*

The journey God has your best interest in mind for your journey, even though there will be diversions along the way.

Pandemic

Widespread diseases are fast-moving among large populations can adversely affect people for generations. This process is not isolated to diseases spread through contact that make people physically ill.

Pornography has become a pandemic with consequences that wreck men, women, children and future generations. Children are exposed at an early age, sex slavery is big business, and sex addicts are being created. The statistics on this topic are staggering. Someone you know may be fighting a battle against this disease.

The Bible says in 1 Corinthians 6:18 (ESV): *"Flee from sexual immorality. Every other sin a person commits is outside the body, but the sexually immoral person sins against his own body."*

Let's pray the hearts and minds of the people who are battling this disease will come to understand the true destruction happening each time they use the highly addictive drug called pornography.

October 20th

Unfamiliar Territory

Many people have comfort zones in which they like to operate. Occasionally, they will find the need to venture outside those zones for events or requirements for work, school or pleasure.

Moses led the Israelites out of Egypt and into the wilderness in the Old Testament, and nobody knew exactly where their journey would end. The people still chose to follow Moses into the wilderness.

The Bible says in Deuteronomy 1:30-31 (NASB): *"The Lord your God who goes before you will Himself fight on your behalf, just as He did for you in Egypt before your eyes, and in the wilderness where you saw how the Lord your God carried you, just as a man carries his son, in all the way which you have walked until you came to this place."*

Whatever unfamiliar surroundings are present in your life, know that God is always right there with you.

Prayer of the Week

Luke 18:1 (NIV)

"Then Jesus told his disciples a parable to show them that they should always pray and not give up."

Pray about your concerns this week, this month, this year, this decade and until you hear from God about what to do in relation to those issues.

October 22nd

Shine Bright

When you became a Christian, God lit your pilot light with an eternal flame powered by the Holy Spirit. You may be a baby, an adolescent or an adult in your faith.

No matter where you are in your faith, the evil one will try to extinguish that flame. Sometimes Christians make the work easy by hiding the light or smoldering the flame that once burned bright. This happens with sin and distancing yourself from the Spirit and God.

Jesus says in Luke 11:36 (NASB): *"If therefore your whole body is full of light, with no dark part in it, it will be wholly illumined, as when the lamp illumines you with its rays."*

Stay close to God, allowing your light to shine brightly in this dark world.

October 23rd

Praise and Worship

What music fills the speakers of your vehicle, your earbuds and the stereo in your home? Research shows the type of music you listen to changes your mood and can affect the way you perceive the world. (Visit ScienceDaily.com to read an article on this topic.)

My vehicle's radio is preset to local Christian stations, which is uplifting during travels. You can also search for a K-Love or Air1 radio station for positive music with a biblical message.

The Bible says in Colossians 3:16 (NIV): *"Let the message of Christ dwell among you richly as you teach and admonish one another with all wisdom through psalms, hymns and songs from the Spirit, singing to God with gratitude in your hearts."*

I challenge you to listen to Christian radio for the next 30 days and notice the change in your attitude, mood and perception of the world around you.

October 24th

Smoke Detectors

When you are living in the Spirit and sin shows up in your life, it should set off an alarm like a smoke detector. The purpose of the alert is two-fold: to make it known there is a fire breaking out; and to extinguish the flames before they are out of control.

When sin first enters your life, you should be alerted and take preventative measures to put out the flames of desire, hate, anger or whatever sin you are battling. Sin, when put out quickly, is easier to fight than when it becomes a raging fire in your heart and mind.

The Bible says in 1 Peter 1:13 (NLT): *"So prepare your minds for action and exercise self-control. Put all your hope in the gracious salvation that will come to you when Jesus Christ is revealed in the world."*

Make a habit of checking your internal detectors for sin regularly so you can douse the flames before they are out of control.

October 25th

Guideposts

Streets, highways and roads across most of the populated world have signs directing you toward cities, towns, government buildings and historical sites. Many can be confusing when you are new to an area. When hiking, markers keep you on the path and oriented, so you don't end up in a dangerous situation.

These signs guide you to your selected destinations unless the primitive signage wears off and paths are not well designated, which can confuse even the best navigators.

The Bible says in Psalm 25:4 (NLT): *"Show me the fight path, O Lord; point out the road for me to follow."*

Always allow God to be your navigator through life and stay on the correct path, leading to the destinations He has for you.

Mulligan

The term mulligan in sports – especially golf – grants a player the opportunity to take a second attempt for a more desirable outcome. It is considered a do-over without penalty strokes or any adverse effect on the overall score.

Is there time in life when you want a second, third or even fourth attempt to make something right or achieve a goal? Although second chances are not always available, forgiveness is better than a mulligan.

Jesus talks about the prodigal son in Luke 15:11-32 (NIV): *"But we had to celebrate and be glad because this brother of yours was dead and is alive again; he was lost and is found."*

God knows we need second chances, but we must turn from our sins to God for that forgiveness.

Anno Domini

A.D. (n.d.) means in the year of our Lord. Before the late 20th century, the Latin abbreviations B.C. and A.D. designated the times before Christ and after death. To avoid offending non-Christians, the terms were updated to BCE, Before the Common Era, and CE, Common Era.

The terms can be changed to whatever, by whomever and to whatever the powers that be deem appropriate for all people. The fact remains: Jesus plays a defining role in the entire world, so much so that eras are divided into before Him and after He was here on earth as a man sent from God to save the world.

Jesus says in Matthew 28:20 (NASB): *"Teaching them to observe all that I commanded you; and lo, I am with you always, even to the end of the age."*

The power of Jesus Christ is stronger than any term the world places upon His Holy name. Let's continue to love, worship and praise our God.

October 28th

Prayer of the Week

Psalm 67:1 (NASB)

"God be gracious to us and bless us and make His face shine upon us, Selah."

Pray to God for our nation this week and that His will be done in all things.

October 29th

Pollution

The image of pollution is waste floating in rivers, streams and the ocean or the smog from manufacturing. The damage to our earth impacts people, plants and animals.

Something just as destructive comes out of people's mouths. Hateful words can damage the person who hears them.

Jesus says in Matthew 15:11 (NLT): *"It's not what goes into your mouth that defiles you; you are defiled by the words that come out of your mouth."*

We can each do our part to clean up the world by sharing caring and kind words to foster an environment filled with love.

October 30th

Be Still

Duty calls us to wear different hats throughout the day, week, month and year…putting out fires at work, helping the kids with homework, preparing meals for the family and more.

When is there time to rest from all these activities? Remember: we are not God – even He rested.

The Bible says in Psalm 46:10 (NIV): *"He says, 'Be still, and know that I am God; I will be exalted among the nations, I will be exalted in the earth.'"*

Take time to hit the pause button on life, relax for a few moments, breathe and clear your mind.

October 31st

Halloween

Today is a day of dressing up in costumes, having parties, carving faces into pumpkins and, for children, going trick or treating to collect candy. Long before the commercialization of this day, Christians prayed, fasted and held vigils for the dead. Some believe Halloween is a Christian holiday (Halloween, n.d.).

A horror movie series bears the name and most of us associate Halloween with scary tales and creepy happenings. Evil lurks once the sun goes down.

The Bible says in 3 John 1:11 (NLT): *"Dear friend, don't let this bad example influence you. Follow only what is good. Remember that those who do good prove that they are God's children and those who do evil prove that they do not know God."*

Keep every day honest and pure in thoughts and actions toward your fellow man.

November

November 1st

The Winning Team

Everyone wants to play for a winning team. There are times when we decide to play for the underdog, thinking there is a chance to win an inning or score a goal. But the end is always the same. We think if we choose a side, God will join us – not the other way around.

You can have the ultimate victory by choosing the greatest team of all time.

The Bible says in Romans 8:31 (ESV): *"What shall we say to these things? If God is for us, who can be against us?"*

God is always for us when we are playing for His team.

November 2nd

Editor's Choice

As I prepared to submit this book of daily devotions, I contemplated which publishing company to use with limited financial resources to allocate for the production. I thought about posting on social media to find an editor. Within minutes of this thought, a friend and editor walked through the door. We spoke about the matter and came to an agreement.

Jesus says in Matthew 7:8 (ESV): *"For everyone who asks receives, and the one who seeks finds, and to the one who knocks it will be opened."*

Allow God to be the editor of your story.

November 3rd

Well Done

Doesn't it feel great to have a teacher, manager, coach, parent or peer tell that you did a great job with the responsibilities that were trusted to you. Even more so, that you will be entrusted with more and greater things because of your dedication and diligence with minor matters.

The Bibles says in Matthew 25:23 (NLT): *'Well done, my good and faithful servant. You have been faithful in handling this small amount, so now I will give you many more responsibilities. Let's celebrate together!'*

Do what God has trusted you to do here on earth so when the day comes to see Him face to face you will hear Him say "Well Done!"

November 4th

Prayer of the Week

Psalm 43:3 (NIV)

"Send me your light and your faithful care, let them lead me; let them bring me to your holy mountain, to the place where you dwell."

Pray that God will guide you in all you do this week.

November 5th

No Words

Have you ever been at a loss for words after shocking news, a surprise or witnessing the birth of a baby?

When praying to God, you may be unable to clearly articulate your thoughts. The Holy Spirit always knows your heart and thoughts.

The Bible says in Romans 8:26 (NIV): *"In the same way, the Spirit helps us in our weakness. We do not know what we ought to pray for, but the Spirit himself intercedes for us through wordless groans."*

Pour out your heart to God even though you are unable to speak!

November 6th

Blessed Work

Long days don't necessarily equate to more money or more blessings from God. There is plenty of work to be done, but all in due time. Having a backlog of work is better than having no work at all.

My former career kept me on the road for extended periods of time and the days were long. Following the Lord fully wasn't a top priority and, eventually, the end of the road came. When I started working for God, He poured out His blessings.

The Bible says in Psalm 127:2 (NET): *"It is vain for you to rise early, come home late, and work so hard for your food. Yes, He can provide for those whom He loves even when they sleep."*

Be blessed because of how you labor, not because of your labor.

November 7th

Leader to Follow

Throughout history, Hitler, Stalin and Pol Pot are examples of leaders who we should not follow. These are extreme cases and easy to distinguish. However, there are organizations, businesses, groups, celebrities and other people in leadership roles who do not display behaviors worthy of being followed.

On the other hand, there are examples of great leaders such as Abraham Lincoln, Mahatma Gandhi and Mother Teresa. You may find amazing leaders at work, school and church.

The Bible says in Hebrews 13:7 (NASB): *"Remember those who led you, who spoke the word of God to you; and considering the result of their conduct, imitate their faith."*

Find a leader who exudes the qualities of Jesus as an example to follow!

November 8th

Loving, Living and Leading Like Jesus

Is mankind capable of being Christlike? Many people will tell you it is impossible. When you witness examples of people being the hands and feet of Jesus while living in the spirit, you will know without doubt it is possible.

Where mankind gets it wrong is selfishly inserting themselves into the mix, as if they are someone to be praised. God uses anyone who is willing to empty themselves so the Holy Spirit can work in and through man.

The Bible says in 1 John 2:5 (NLT): *"But those who obey God's word truly show how completely they love Him. That is how we know we are living in Him."*

Allow the Holy Spirit to work in and through you in all aspects of your life and show the world the Love of God.

Step of Faith

People who jump out of a plane with a parachute or step off a platform to zip across a steel cable have some level of faith. There is faith in whoever packed the parachute and in those who maintain the zipline cable.

My wife and I went ziplining to get a different view of God's wonderful creation. Some of the platforms were high above the ground. Although I do not fear heights, it was startling to see how far down it was if something went wrong. It reminded me God is with me in times when I'm apprehensive. So, I stepped off the ledge.

The Bible says in Isaiah 41:10 (NIV): *"So do not fear, for I am with you; do not be dismayed, for I am your God. I will strengthen you; I will uphold you with my righteous right hand."*

Place your faith in God to watch over and protect you.

November 10th

Truth and Righteousness

Your enemy, the devil, will distort the truth and dishonor everything, leaving a path of destruction in its wake. The best way to do battle is to use the Bible to stand firm against Satan's evil schemes.

The Bible says in Ephesians 6:14 (ESV): *"Stand therefore, having fastened on the belt of truth, and having put on the breastplate of righteousness."*

Stay in the word of God in times of peace so you are prepared for war.

November 11th

Prayer of the Week

John 14:13 (NIV)

"And I will do whatever you ask in my name, so that the Father may be glorified in the Son."

Practice praying to do God's will in and through your life, so He is the one receiving all the glory for the things you do.

November 12th

Continuing Education

School for American students of all ages is in full swing this time of year. Young adults' study in college while other men and women make career advancements, hoping to make their dreams come true.

Whatever your stage of life, one thing should be consistent: education doesn't stop when you reach a certain age, degree status or income level. Learning should be part of your existence, especially learning from God and His teachings.

The Bible says in Proverbs 2:6 (NASB): *"For the Lord gives wisdom; from His mouth come knowledge and understanding."*

Continue to learn all the days of your life!

November 13th

Common Bond

Everyone wants to be unique or set apart from the rest of the world. Instead of looking for differences that make us unique and striving for ways to distance ourselves from everyone else, we should look for what bond us in unity.

Relationships normally start when two or more people have something in common. We are meant for relationships. Seek a commonality upon which to build a relationship.

Proverbs 22:2 (NIV) says: *"Rich and poor have this in common: The Lord is the Maker of them all."*

Focus on ways to bond together, instead of how to separate from the group.

November 14th

In Awe of All

Go to a peaceful place and take the time to observe all God has created and given you. Focus on the blessing alone. Time may slip away as you begin to reflect on everything.

The Bible says in Acts 2:43 (NASB): *"Everyone kept feeling a sense of awe; and many wonders and signs were taking place through the apostles."*

You can feel this sense of awe when you examine all your blessings!

Necessities

What do you need to survive in the world? You may need to sit down for this, because a smartphone, electricity, clean clothes, fast food, cable television and the internet didn't make the list. Water, food, shelter and clothing are the basic needs of every person.

While in the African bush with a mission team, we had water, food and shelter provided. The water was filtered because it was not clean. Ugali was a staple food and meat came from locally raised animals. Our shelter was tenting to protect us from mosquitoes and rain. We survived and were happy with what God gave us.

Jesus says in Matthew 6:25 (NLT): *"That is why I tell you not to worry about everyday life – whether you have enough food and drink, or enough clothes to wear. Isn't life more than food, and your body more than clothing?"*

God provides the necessities, not the amenities.

November 16th

Combat Preparedness

How ready are you to fight your greatest enemy, the devil? The evil one is always prepared to wage war against you and will use anything in his arsenal.

Many of us wage war with evil underprepared or not at all. The evil one has an easy job when we are not prepared. The devil will go after the strongest to prove a point too. In recent headlines, Hillsong artist Marty Sampson renounced his faith.

The Bible says in Ephesians 6:11(NIV): *"Put on the full armor of God, so that you can take your stand against the devil's schemes."*

Pray for the hearts and minds of fellow Christians to be prepared for the battles that test faith.

Living Forever

Some people believe they live one life and die…the end. They may live to the fullest, enjoying whatever they desire with no regard for anyone else. It is sad to see the rush to fill life with excitement and despair from nothing to anticipate.

Does this sound like you? This describes my rebellious years. My lack of knowledge and understanding was the devil's playground.

Satan likes to make us feel this life is it and nothing we say or do can prevent death. God tells us otherwise. Once we gain this knowledge and accept Christ into our lives, the evil one loses control.

The Bible says in 1 John 2:17 (NIV): *"The world and its desires pass away, but whoever does the will of God lives forever."*

Doing God's will be the first step to living in His presence for eternity.

November 18th

Prayer of the Week

Colossians 4:2 (NASB)

"Devote yourselves to prayer, keeping alert in it with an attitude of thanksgiving."

Pray like you have never prayed before and do so with a grateful heart.

November 19th

Trials and Tribulations

Everyone can expect to face trials and tribulations. Even Jesus faced extreme adversity while He was on Earth. As Christians, we have hope in the outcome when God's purposes are accomplished.

Your difficulties are unique and whether you address them with great hope or great despair says much about your character. The non-believer may see every trial as hopeless, but we have hope in Jesus Christ.

The Bible says in Romans 5:3-5 (ESV): *"Not only that, but we rejoice in our sufferings, knowing that suffering produces endurance, and endurance produces character, and character produces hope, and hope does not put us to shame, because God's love has been poured into our hearts through the Holy Spirit who had been given to us."*

God is immersed in all you are going through, so keep hope alive in your heart.

November 20ᵗʰ

Peace, Love and Worship

It has been more than 50 years since a festival called Woodstock changed the face of music. Nearly 500,000 individuals came together peacefully to listen to the greatest musicians of their time. The celebration was filled with peace, love and music, along with recreational drugs that remain mostly illegal.

Let me take you back to the beginning of the church. There were not as many people on the day of Pentecost, but God was in their midst. On that day alone, nearly 3,000 people accepted Christ and were filled with the Holy Spirit. The celebration hasn't stopped since its birth more than 2,000 years ago.

The Bible says in Acts 2:47 (NLT): *"All the while praising God and enjoying the goodwill of all the people. And each day the Lord added to their fellowship those who were being saved."*

You too can be part of the kingdom that is filled with people who love one another! Pray this prayer: Lord, I am a sinner, I accept that Jesus lived, died and has risen for my sins so I can be with you in eternity. I know in my heart that Jesus Christ is my Savior. I invite the Holy Spirit into my life to guide me on the path you have for me. I thank you and praise you. In Jesus' name I pray, Amen!

November 21st

Superstition

Many people, including Christians, fall prey to superstitions. Some believe the number 13 is bad – often hotels don't have a 13th floor. Fans and athletes might think a pair of lucky socks leads to a better performance.

While growing up, I was vulnerable to superstitions and may still have some. Growing in wisdom from the Bible helped me realize my superstitions put my faith in an object or thing over my God.

The Bible says in 1 Timothy 4:7 (ESV): *"Have nothing to do with irreverent, silly myths. Rather train yourself for godliness."*

Place your faith and trust in God, not that lucky charm.

November 22nd

Redemption

We all have sin in our lives – we can't make ourselves right by any amount of good works. No amount of money can purchase our way out of the guilty verdict. Satan wants us to think we can't be saved. Knowing Jesus Christ allows us to see through the author of lies.

The Bible says in Romans 3:24 (NLT): *"Yet God, in His grace, freely makes us right in His sight. He did this through Christ Jesus when He freed us from the penalty for our sins."*

You can receive this gift and know that no matter your past, you are redeemed. Pray this prayer: Lord, I am a sinner. I accept that Jesus lived, died and has risen for my sins so that I can be with you in eternity. I know in my heart that Jesus Christ is my Savior. I invite the Holy Spirit into my life to guide me on the path you have for me. I thank you and praise you. In Jesus' name I pray, Amen!

Welcome to the kingdom. My prayer is you will be redeemed or share this with someone who needs to be.

November 23rd

Personal Responsibility

Look around and you see individuals blaming anyone but themselves for a problem. You may have passed on blame to somebody else to avoid punishment, fear or shame.

If you struggle with this sin, it is time to stop and seek help. If not, pray for softening hearts and minds in people who desperately need guidance, salvation and a clear picture of reality. Get involved and be part of the solution, guiding and mentoring those who are uneducated about the consequences of personal responsibility.

The Bible says in 2 Corinthians 5:10 (NASB): *"For we must all appear before the judgment seat of Christ, so that each one may be recompensed for his deeds in the body, according to what he has done, whether good or bad."*

Allow the Holy Spirit to guide you on the journey of recovery or mentoring others.

November 24th

The Heart

The heart muscle pumps blood throughout the body to keep up alive. The blood must be free of impurities to provide nourishment to our organs. Blood filled with impurities like alcohol and drugs can damage the organs and destroy them.

Medical research shows stress, anger and other negative emotions can also have devastating effects on the human body.

The Bible says in Proverbs 4:23 (NIV): *"Above all else, guard your heart, for everything you do flows from it."*

Be sure to keep your heart pumping positive thoughts and clean blood to the rest of your body.

November 25th

Prayer of the Week

Psalm 143:1 (NIV)

"Lord, hear my prayer, listen to my cry for mercy; in your faithfulness and righteousness come to my relief."

Pray this week for rescue from the things that keep you up at night and for rest to replace the worry and distress.

November 26th

Thanksgiving

The last Thursday of November is Thanksgiving Day in the United States of America. Other countries also celebrate a similar holiday for giving thanks, praying and feasting.

Families gather, watch football, overeat and look at deals for the opening of holiday shopping. Thankfulness can get lost in all the other day's activities.

The Bible says in Psalm 136:26 (NLT): *"Give thanks to the God of heaven. His faithful love endures forever."*

Give thanks to God every day for the blessings He gives you.

November 27th

Constantly Seeking

Is there anything you find yourself constantly doing? Parents care for children, farmers plant and harvest, and these days, most of us stare at our mobile devices.

So many prefer hiding from the truth by seeking distractions over seeking guidance or growth. By seeking your heavenly Father, you can begin to understand what you are here to do and bring greater meaning to your life.

The Bible says in 1 Chronicles 16:11 (NLT): *"Search for the Lord and for His strength; continually seek Him."*

Make continually seeking God in all you do a priority every day.

November 28th

Black Friday

The day after Thanksgiving in America is one of the biggest shopping days of the year. People shop all night hours for deals on stuff they think will bring happiness to their loved ones at Christmas. Often, chaos surrounds the best buys. Shoppers want the latest and greatest gifts and go extremes to acquire them.

The Bible says in 1 John 2:16 (NLT): *"For the world offers only a craving for physical pleasure, a craving for everything we see, and pride in our achievements and possessions. These are not from the Father but are from this world."*

Have a healthy perspective of the reason for the season as you go about your gift-giving.

November 29th

Trust

Have you ever put your faith in someone or something besides God? How did it work out?

We often substitute an object or person into a place where only God should be. This misplaced trust may hinder any progress we're working toward – or result in complete failure.

The Bible says in Proverbs 3:6 (NASB): *"In all your ways acknowledge Him, and He will make our paths straight."*

Always trust in God for everything and He will keep your progress moving in the right direction.

Fill My Heart

Within our hearts, we all have the will to do something – make millions, be a professional athlete or make a difference in the community.

Free will allows each of us to decide how we fill our minds and hearts. Push out selfish ambitions and be filled with God's will for you.

The Bible says in Psalm 40:8 (NIV): *"I desire to do your will, my God; your law is within my heart."*

Allow your heart to be filled with the desires God has for you because His perfect will is better than you can imagine.

December

December 1st

Farsighted

Have you met someone who is farsighted? Not in relation to their vision, but someone who sees what is wrong with everyone else, but not within themselves?

We think we see others clearly, but it is difficult to look in the mirror and see ourselves. Changing our visual field about others may be the prescription we need.

The Bible says in Matthew 7:2 (NIV): *"For in the same way you judge others, you will be judged, and with the measure you use, it will be measured you."*

Change your prescription for how you view others.

December 2nd

Prayer of the Week

Psalm 85:7 (NIV)

"Show us your unfailing love, Lord, and grant us your salvation."

Each of us can be our own worst enemy needing to be saved from self-destruction. Pray the Lord will rescue you from yourself.

December 3rd

Day of Pentecost

Jesus promised after He was gone the Holy Spirit would come to help the Apostles.

Acts 2:4 (NLT) says: *"And everyone present was filled with the Holy Spirit and began speaking in other languages, as the Holy Spirit gave them this ability."*

Allow the Holy Spirit to fill you with the love and peace of Christ.

December 4th

Be A Blessing

Do you give money, time or an ear to listen with abundance or do you withhold all of these like Ebenezer Scrooge in "A Christmas Carol" by Charles Dickens? Ebenezer was ruthless in his business dealings and the way he treated his employees but had a change of heart when he saw things from another perspective.

When you give, do so without an expectation of receiving anything in return. The act becomes a loan when you expect something back, thus negating the blessing.

Jesus says in Luke 6:38 (NIV): *"Give, and it will be given to you. A good measure, pressed down, shaken together and running over, will be poured into your lap. For with the measure you use, it will be measured to you."*

Bless others with abundantly and you, in turn, will be blessed.

December 5th

Do You See Love?

Look at who and what are in your surroundings. Are there loving and compassionate people in your life, or those filled with hate and strife?

People filled with hate tend to surround themselves with hate. People who have love, spread love to those around them and attract others who love.

The Bible says in Colossians 3:14 (NLT): *"Above all, clothe yourselves with love, which binds us all together in perfect harmony."*

Spread love with all you encounter today!

December 6th

Greatest Treasure

Most people know of the greatest treasure, but do not to accept it. Others wait hear of this treasure. If you have heard the gospel of Jesus Christ, what are you doing with it? Are you burying it, investing it or proclaiming it to the non-believing world? The treasure of the gospel is meant to be shared, not buried.

2nd Timothy 1:14 (NASB) says: *"Guard, through the Holy Spirit who dwells in us, the treasure which has been entrusted to you."*

Share the gospel – those who accept it will be thankful you shared the treasure with them.

December 7th

Nearsighted

Sight is a precious sense many take for granted – in both the physical and spiritual worlds.

Are you diligent in growing your faith? Do you live out your faith? As believers growing in faith, we again knowledge, self-control, perseverance, godliness, kindness and love, according to the Bible.

2 Peter 1:9 (ESV) says: *"For whoever lacks these qualities is so nearsighted that he is blind, having forgotten that he was cleansed from his former sins."*

Take care of your physical and spiritual sight as you grow in faith.

December 8th

Glorify the Father

Do you do good works only for recognition, or do your good works allow others to see God's glory in what you do? It is ok to receive recognition for your accomplishments. However, credit should go to the One who helps you do good.

Many will accept all the credit for a project, an accomplishment or a good deed without showing respect to other team members or God.

Jesus says in Matthew 5:16 (NIV): *"In the same way, let your light shine before others, that they may see your good deeds and glorify your Father in heaven."*

Give credit where credit is due.

December 9th

Prayer of the Week

1 Timothy 2:8 (NLT)

"In every place of worship, I want men to pray with holy hands lifted up to God, free from anger and controversy."

As we reach the end of the year, you now have a better idea how to pray. This week be a leader in prayer at your place of worship and do so with a loving heart.

December 10th

Jesus Weeps

The world is hurting, and it is painful to watch people bring misery on themselves with their free will. We each make decisions that have a lasting impact on ourselves and those around us.

Some are dealt a hand they did not choose. When you see starving orphans, refugees displaced by war or exploited children, you may weep.

The Bible says in John 11:35 (NASB): *"Jesus wept."*

We should pray and take actions to help heal people who are hurting.

December 11th

Father's Day

Some parents are not present in their children's lives for various reasons, while others are present and active. No matter what category you fall into, you have a heavenly Father who loves you and wants to be part of your life in a meaningful way.

The Bible says in Proverbs 3:12 (NLT): *"For the Lord corrects those he loves, just as a father corrects a child in whom he delights."*

Be sure to give thanks to your earthly father, as well as your heavenly Father.

December 12th

God is Watching

We are required to obey the laws where we live. You may disagree with speed limit laws, for example, but will pay the price of a ticket if officials catch you disobeying.

Some laws throughout the world are similar, but punishment varies widely. In the United States, the punishment for theft varies from probation to a long prison sentence, depending on circumstances surrounding the crime. In other countries, punishment can be the loss of a hand.

The Bible says in Ecclesiastes 12:14 (NASB): *"For God will bring every act to judgment, everything which is hidden, whether it is good and evil."*

Ask God to forgive you of your sins – seen and unseen.

December 13th

Encouragement and Assistance

On a walking along the bike path near my home, a friend and I encountered a homeless man named Rich. We spoke with Rich, learned his story and then prayed for him.

Rich lost his home, his health and battles alcohol and tobacco addiction along with depression. He said he and wants to go be with Jesus. We provided Rich with local non-profit help center info and offered to take him there, but he declined.

Many people like Rich need someone to listen and encourage them. You may know someone just like him.

The Bible says in Psalm 46:1 (NLT): *"God is our refuge and strength, always ready to help in times of trouble."*

Please pray for people like Rich who need to accept God's help.

December 14th

What Time Is It?

Seconds, minutes, hours, days, weeks, months, years, decades are ways we measure time. Anticipating a vacation seems to take eternity, then it passes too briefly.

Most adults agree time passes more quickly as we age. Time is precious, yet so many wastes it – enjoy all the ups and downs of life because each moment is fleeting.

The Bible says in Ecclesiastes 3:4 (NASB): *"A time to weep and a time to laugh; a time to mourn and a time to dance."*

Wherever you are in at this moment, pause and give thanks to the Lord for this time.

December 15th

Count to Three

Having a positive attitude in all areas of life is important but can be difficult when negativity permeates your outlook.

The Bible says in 1 Thessalonians 5:19 (NASB): *"Do not quench the Spirit."*

Count at least three blessings in your life right now. Stay in the Holy Spirit, stay positive.

December 16th

Prayer of the Week

Hebrews 4:15 (NLT)

"This High Priest of ours understands our weaknesses, for He faced all of the same testing's we do, yet He did not sin."

You prayed to a magnificent God this year who faced the same temptations as you. Take time this week to reflect on all the prayers you prayed and give thanks to the Son of God for breaking down the wall down used to separate us from Him.

December 17ᵗʰ

Looking Forward to Summer

In the Northern Hemisphere, summer is a distant memory, but longing for it can be as intense as the cold, windy weather.

Sports, vacations, outdoor activities and other adventures fill the summer months. It is also important to keep God in focus during these busy times.

The Bible says in Ecclesiastes 3:1 (NLT): *"For everything, there is a season, a time for every activity under heaven."*

Enjoy the present season of life – it will change before you know it

December 18th

Cheerful Giving

Do you give to the poor, the church, a person in need? If so, do you give out of guilt, for something in return or to gain grace from God? Giving brings great joy to the giver if it is done with the right attitude.

When giving becomes a chore done with reluctance, it becomes nothing more than an obligation. God wants you to give with great delight.

The Bible says in 2 Corinthians 9:7 (NASB): *"Each one must do just as he purposed in his heart, not grudgingly or under compulsion for God loves a cheerful giver."*

Giving brings great joy to the giver, receiver and God.

December 19th

Today is the Day

You are here for a purpose. God placed you precisely to accomplish His will in and through your life. Any hardships you face are for your growth.

In Africa, the pastor hosting us sang a verse and song from the book of Psalms. It brightens my mood every time I hear or read it.

The Bible says in Psalm 118:24 (NLT): *"This is the day the Lord has made. We will rejoice and be glad in it."*

God is with you in whatever you are going through, so rejoice and be glad in it.

December 20th

All the Glory

It is upsetting when you work hard, apply yourself and then someone else gets the limelight. Receiving glory is reserved for one and that is where it should go.

The Bible says in 1 Corinthians 10:31 (NIV): *"So whether you eat or drink or whatever you do, do it all for the glory of God."*

Give all the glory to God!

December 21st

Surrender All

Is it hard for you to submit to a higher authority? Control, to an extent, is in our DNA. Some people are control-freaks, while others go with the flow. For most, surrendering all is inconceivable.

The Bible says in Galatians 2:20 (NIV): *"I have been crucified with Christ and I no longer live, but Christ lives in me. The life I now live in the body, I live by faith in the Son of God, who loved me and gave himself for me."*

By releasing control, you release the sinful nature preventing you from experiencing God's fullness for your life. It is difficult, but the resulting discipline is the final reward.

December 22nd

Overcome

At this moment, your difficulties may seem like 20-foot waves crashing on you in the middle of a storm. Once the storm subsides, you reflect upon the situation to see those waves were barely breakers.

Real-world problems result from sin in our lives or from living in a sinful world. No matter the cause, we can limit the effects on us.

Jesus says in John 16:33 (NASB): *"These things I have spoken to you, so that in Me you may have peace. In the world you have tribulation but take courage; I have overcome the world."*

Only God can be your true peace in the middle of the storm, providing a rainbow after it passes.

December 23rd

Prayer of the Week

Colossians 4:2 (NLT)

"Devote yourselves to prayer with an alert mind and a thankful heart."

Give thanks for the birth of Christ as you celebrate Christmas. May all your Christmas prayers be answered according to God's will for your life. Merry Christmas from GIV365!

December 24th

Walking with God

As Christians, it's difficult for us to believe there were people in His time who refused to believe Christ was the son of God. Those men and women were in the presence of Jesus and still did not believe.

We do not have the luxury of seeing God in His physical being, but we have His teachings, His masterful artistry in the sky and all creation. His promises keep us grounded in our faith.

The Bible says in 2 Corinthians 5:7(NASB): *"For we walk by faith, not by sight."*

When we are strong in our faith, we know we are walking with God every day because we have faith in His promises.

December 25th

Christmas

Christians all over the world from every nationality, background and race celebrate the birth of Jesus Christ, the savior of the world. To the non-believing world, it sounds absurd to celebrate such an event, but to those who know and love Him, it makes perfect sense.

The secular world believes it is a time of receiving and giving gifts to show people love. Businesses commercialize the holiday meant for so much more.

The Bible says in Luke 2:11 (NASB): *"For today in the city of David there has been born for you a Savior, who is Christ the Lord."*

Pray with me today thanking God for sending His son to us in human form to be a blessing to all people who come to know Him as their Lord and Savior. Amen.

December 26th

Return of Christ

How do you feel when discussing Christ's return to earth – fear, indifference or great joy?

I once had great fear and anxiety surrounding the second coming of Christ. Growth in knowledge of the love that God has for me, I realize that His return is a glorious moment of great anticipation. Education resulted in greater knowledge and understanding.

The Bible says in Revelation 19:1 (NLT): *"After this, I heard what sounded like a vast crowd in heaven shouting, 'Praise the Lord! Salvation and glory and power belong to our God.'"*

There is no fear in knowing God is coming back to make all things right and whole.

December 27th

Their Shoes

We all encounter conflict. What seems trivial to one is a major obstacle for another to overcome.

Walking in someone else's shoes is a great way to comprehend their struggle. In Living Water of Ohio's 1st Annual Walk for Water, 70 people experienced the plight of Africans retrieving water for cleaning and cooking. Participants from age 2 to mid-70s walked 1.5 miles to retrieve water and carry it back to the starting point.

The Bible says in Galatians 6:2 (NIV): *"Carry each other's burdens, and in this way, you will fulfill the law of Christ."*

Take a moment to think about someone who may be struggling. Try to see the obstacles they face from their perspective and then share in their burden.

December 28th

Tested

Have you encountered a screaming child, a traffic jam when running late or any other experiences that try your patience? Maybe God is testing you during those times. Looking back, would you say you passed or failed the test?

When God places a test before you to measure your relationship with Him, you may find you still have some growing to do spiritually.

The Bible says in James 1:12 (NLT): *"God blesses those who patiently endure testing and temptation. Afterward they will receive the crown of life that God has promised to those who love Him."*

Constantly study God's word so you will be prepared for any test He assigns you.

December 29th

In My Absence

Some of you may have noticed that there have not been any new daily devotionals published over the past week. This week has been filled with a final in my first semester of the Master of Ministry and the completion of the editing for the GIV365 devotional book. Not that there are excuses being made for my absence, but school and publishing the book have taken precedence.

I hope that in the meantime you have taken the opportunity to browse 300+ devotionals on social media to date. The hope is to be back at the daily devotions as soon as possible.

The Bible says in Colossians 2:5 (NASB): *"For even though I am absent in body, nevertheless I am with you in spirit, rejoicing to see your good discipline and the stability of your faith in Christ."*

Know that even though people are not present with you, they are still with you in spirit.

December 30th

Prayer of the Week

Ecclesiastes 7:8 (NASB)

"The end of a matter is better than its beginning; patience of spirit is better than haughtiness of spirit."

As you close out the year, pray for all that has been endured and accomplished this year. Pray for a spiritual calming of the mind as you embark on a new chapter. Amen.

December 31st

Fearless

The Bible states 365 times not to fear – that just happens to be the same number of days in a calendar year (except leap year). God wants us to know we do not need to be afraid and for good reason. He was with us yesterday, today and tomorrow and for eternity.

Overcoming fear may seem impossible to those in its grip. I used to have plenty of fear to share – producing this book gave me some fear. But I know God is with me, guiding me every step of the way. The words in this book, after all, are His. I am just the hands and feet of Jesus and so are you.

The Bible says in Mark 6:50 (NLT): *"They were all terrified when they saw him. But Jesus spoke to them at once. 'Don't be afraid,' He said. 'Take courage! I am here.'"*

As we close out this book and year, know that God wants all of us to feel His loving presence and be FEARLESS all the days of our lives!

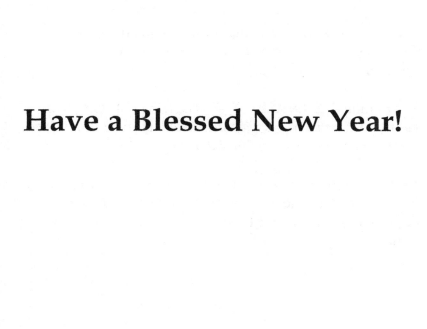

Have a Blessed New Year!

February 29th

Tag, You're It

Remember playing tag as a child or even now with children or grandchildren? Let's play it now!

Somewhere, someone – maybe you – needs to hear that God loves them. Tag as many people you can and share on your social media for all to see.

Zephaniah 3:17 (NASB) says: *"The Lord your God is in your midst, a victorious warrior. He will be quiet in His love; He will rejoice over you with shouts of joy."*

Pray that whoever reads this will understand that God loves them for who they are and in whatever circumstance they find themselves in this moment. Amen.

References

A.D. (n.d.). Wikipedia the free encyclopedia. Retrieved from https://www.dictionary.com/

Amen. (n.d.). In Dictionary online. Retrieved https://www.dictionary.com/

Cohen, D. (2016). Selfies, narcissism, and social media (infographic). Adweek. Retrieved from https://www.adweek.com/

Global cosmetics products market expected to reach USD 805.61 billion by 2023 – Industry size & share analysis. (2018). Reuters. Retrieved from https://www.reuters.com/

Gluttony. (n.d.). Wikipedia the free encyclopedia. Retrieved from https://www.dictionary.com/

Grace. (n.d.) Wikipedia the free encyclopedia. Retrieved from https://www.dictionary.com/

Halloween. (n.d.). Wikipedia the free encyclopedia.

Retrieved from https://en.wikipedia.org/

Holst, A. (2019). How many people have smartphones

worldwide? Retrieved from

https://www.statista.com/

In a Year. (n.d.). Open Doors. Retrieved from

https://www.opendoorsusa.org/

In God We Trust. (n.d.). The people history. Retrieved

fromhttp://www.thepeoplehistory.com/july11

th.html

Jim Rohn Quotes. (n.d.). Goodreads. Retrieved from

https://www.goodreads.com/

Jones, J.M. (2013). In U.S., 40% get less than

recommended amount of sleep. Retrieved from

https://news.gallup.com/

Latimer, J. (Producer). (2018, May 1). Quick Talk
Podcast [Audio podcast]. Retrieved
from https://quicktalkpodcast.com/myron-
golden-teaches-us-how-to-make-millions/

Legacy. (n.d.) Wikipedia the free encyclopedia.
Retrieved from https://www.dictionary.com/

List of selfie-related injuries and deaths. (n.d.).
Wikipedia the free encyclopedia. Retrieved from
https://en.wikipedia.org/

Ownership. (n.d.). Wikipedia the free encyclopedia.
Retrieved from https://www.dictionary.com/

Patient. (n.d.) Wikipedia the free encyclopedia.
Retrieved from https://www.dictionary.com/

People spend most of their waking hours staring at
screens. (2018). MarketWatch. Retrieved from
https://www.marketwatch.com/

Role model. (n.d.) Wikipedia the free encyclopedia.

    Retrieved from https://www.dictionary.com/

Stanley, A. (2011). *Enemies of the heart: breaking free from*

    the four emotions that control you. Colorado

    Springs: Multnomah Books.

Time spent working by full- and part-time status,

    gender, and location in 2014. (2015). Retrieved

    from https://www.bls.gov/

Tozer, A. W., & Snyder, J. L. (2014). *The crucified life: how*

    to live out a deeper Christian experience.

    Minneapolis, Minnesota.: Bethany House.

Value of life. (n.d.) Wikipedia the free encyclopedia.

    Retrieved from https://en.wikipedia.org/

Yosemite Sequoias need fire. (n.d.) National

Geographic. Retrieved from

https://video.nationalgeographic.com/video/0

0000144-0a36-d3cb-a96c-7b3f65710000

43685680R00213